Alfred Jackson Lewis

ART IN AMERICA
In Modern Times

The material in this book forms the basis of a series of radio broadcasts over Station WJZ and a coast-to-coast network, through the facilities of the National Broadcasting Company, on Saturday nights from October 6th, 1934, through January 26th, 1935, at 8:00 P.M. Eastern Standard Time; 7:00 P.M. Central Standard Time; 6:00 P.M. Mountain Standard Time; 5:00 P.M. Pacific Standard Time.

ART
IN AMERICA

IN MODERN TIMES

EDITED BY

HOLGER CAHILL
AND ALFRED H. BARR, JR.

REYNAL & HITCHCOCK

New York

THE PLAN FOR THIS SURVEY

WAS INITIATED BY

THE GENERAL FEDERATION OF WOMEN'S CLUBS

UNDER THE AUSPICES OF

THE AMERICAN FEDERATION OF ARTS

WITH THE COOPERATION OF

THE ART INSTITUTE OF CHICAGO

THE METROPOLITAN MUSEUM OF ART

THE MUSEUM OF MODERN ART

THE NATIONAL ADVISORY COUNCIL
ON RADIO IN EDUCATION

THE NATIONAL BROADCASTING COMPANY

Foreword

IN RECENT years fundamental changes in the economic structure of our lives compelled us to pause and to reflect. More and more we became aware that we had placed too much confidence in the returns of material success and realized that we must turn to values that are independent of the fluctuations of prosperity.

In recognition of this need increasing numbers of us have turned to the arts. A new demand for closer contact with art is manifesting itself throughout the country. Museums show a remarkable growth in their attendance. Libraries are asked to supply more books on art than ever before. New art organizations have sprung up in many communities, and the circle of those who want to acquire a sounder knowledge of art is widening from day to day.

In response to this demand Mrs. Henry B. Ness, chairman of the division of art of the General Federation of Women's Clubs, approached the Carnegie Corporation of New York through the offices of the National Advisory Council on Radio in Education, with the request to finance a national broadcast on art in America.

After having conferred with their advisers the trustees of the Carnegie Corporation of New York made an appropriation and requested the American Federation of Arts to organize this program with the co-operation of the Art Institute of Chicago, the Metropolitan Museum of Art, the Museum of Modern Art, the National Advisory Council on Radio in Education, and the National Broadcasting Company. The direction of the program was assigned to René d' Harnoncourt, assistant to the president of the American Federation of Arts.

The entire project has been divided into two series. The first series, covering art in America from 1600 to 1865, was organized with the co-operation of the Art Institute of Chicago and the Metropolitan Museum of Art. The second series, dealing with art in America from 1865 to the present, has been prepared with the co-operation of the Museum of Modern Art.

Illustrated manuals have been published for use with each of the two series to serve the listener as a guide to and reference book on the subjects in the program. This present volume and the broadcasts covering the period from 1865 to the present have been prepared by the Museum of Modern Art and the authors of the various articles with the co-operation of Miss Dorothy Miller and Miss Sarah Newmeyer.

The enthusiastic response from all over the country proves the timeliness and importance of our project. Nearly a hundred museums and art organizations have endorsed the program and it is due to their active and generous co-operation that we are able to present this manual.

For the loan of plates and photographs, for advice and assistance, we express our sincerest gratitude to:

The Art Institute of Chicago; Addison Gallery of American Art, Andover, Mass.; The Brooklyn Museum; The Metropolitan Museum of Art, New York; The New York Historical Society; The New York Public Library; Whitney Museum of American Art, New York; Allied Artists Corporation; Miss Alice Boughton; The Downtown Gallery; Durand-Ruel, Inc.; Ferargil Galleries; The Jefferson Medical College of Philadelphia; Kennedy & Company; Frederick Keppel & Company; C. W. Kraushaar Art Galleries; William Macbeth, Inc.; Movie Makers; Paramount Pictures Corporation; Raymond & Raymond, Inc.; Valentine Gallery; Weyhe Gallery. For permission to reproduce plates thanks are due the following: *The American Magazine of Art* for plates, pages 17 (upper), 31, 43 (lower), 49 (lower), 55; The Bobbs-Merrill Company for lower plate, page 68, from *American Architecture* by Fiske Kimball, 1928; Ferargil Galleries for lower plate, page 15, from *Albert Pinkham Ryder* by F. N. Price, 1933; Harcourt, Brace & Company for plates, pages 63, 65, from *The Brown Decades* by Lewis Mumford, 1931, and plates, pages 57 (lower), 61 (Sterne), 88 (lower), from *America As Americans See It,* 1932; Houghton Mifflin Company for plates, pages 78, 80, from *Modern Housing* by Catherine Bauer, (on the press); *Hound & Horn* for plates, pages 84, 85, 90; Kraushaar Art Galleries for plates, pages 8, 26 (upper), 28 (upper), from *Modern Art in America* by Walter Pach, 1928; The Macmillan Company for upper plate, page 19, from *The History of American Painting* by Samuel Isham, 1915, and lower plate, page 53, from *The History of American Sculpture* by Lorado Taft, 1930; W. W. Norton & Company for plates, pages 73 (lower), 75 (upper), from *The International Style: Architecture Since 1922* by Hitchcock and Johnson, 1932, and for upper plate, page 68, from *The Story of Architecture in America* by T. E. Tallmadge, 1927; Raymond & Raymond, Inc. and *Vanity Fair* for color plates; Charles Scribner's Sons and the office of the late Cass Gilbert for lower plate, page 69, from the magazine *Architecture; Theatre Arts Monthly* for plates, pages 82 (upper), 83; Whitney Museum of American Art for plate, page 24, from *Thomas Eakins, His Life and Work* by Lloyd Goodrich, 1933, for upper plate, page 38, from *Charles Demuth* by William Murrell, 1931, and for plate, page 47.

F. A. WHITING, PRESIDENT
The American Federation of Arts

Endorsing Organizations and Institutions

American Artists Professional League
American Association of Museums
American Library Association

American Association for Adult
Education
College Art Association

Eastern Arts Association
Southern States Art League
Western Arts Association

Andover, Massachusetts
The Addison Gallery of American Art

Ann Arbor, Michigan
University of Michigan Department of
Fine Arts

Atlanta, Georgia
The High Museum of Art

Aurora, New York
Wells College Department of Fine Arts

Austin, Texas
Texas Fine Arts Association

Baltimore, Maryland
The Baltimore Museum of Art
Enoch Pratt Library

Binghamton, New York
Museum of Fine Arts

Bloomfield Hills, Michigan
The Cranbrook Academy of Art

Boston, Massachusetts
Museum of Fine Arts

Buffalo, New York
Albright Art Gallery

Burlington, Vermont
Robert Hull Fleming Museum

Cambridge, Massachusetts
The Fogg Art Museum

Cedar Rapids, Iowa
The Little Gallery

Cincinnati, Ohio
The Cincinnati Art Museum

Cleveland, Ohio
The Cleveland Museum of Art

Columbus, Ohio
The Columbus Gallery of Fine Arts

Davenport, Iowa
Davenport Municipal Art Gallery

Dayton, Ohio
The Dayton Art Institute

Detroit, Michigan
The Detroit Institute of Arts

Elmira, New York
Arnot Art Gallery

Eugene, Oregon
University of Oregon Museum of Art

Flint, Michigan
Flint Institute of Arts

Fort Worth, Texas
Carnegie Public Library

Hagerstown, Maryland
Washington County Museum of Fine
Arts

Hartford, Connecticut
The Wadsworth Athenaeum and Morgan
Memorial

Houston, Texas
The Museum of Fine Arts of Houston

Indianapolis, Indiana
The John Herron Art Institute

Kansas City, Missouri
The William Rockhill Nelson Gallery
of Art

Lawrence, Kansas
The University of Kansas

Los Angeles, California
Los Angeles Museum of History, Science
and Art
Southwest Museum

Louisville, Kentucky
The J. B. Speed Memorial Museum

Manchester, New Hampshire
The Currier Gallery of Art

Memphis, Tennessee
Brooks Memorial Art Gallery
James Lee Memorial Academy of Arts

Mills College P.O., California
Mills College

Milwaukee, Wisconsin
Milwaukee Art Institute
Layton Art Gallery

Minneapolis, Minnesota
The Minneapolis Institute of Arts

Montgomery, Alabama
Montgomery Museum of Fine Arts

Montclair, New Jersey
The Montclair Art Museum

New Britain, Connecticut
Library of the New Britain Institute

Newark, New Jersey
The Newark Museum

New Haven, Connecticut
Yale University School of the Fine Arts

New London, Connecticut
Lyman Allyn Museum

New Orleans, Louisiana
The Isaac Delgado Museum of Art

New York City
Brooklyn Museum
Museum of the City of New York
New York Historical Society
Whitney Museum of American Art

Northampton, Massachusetts
Smith College Museum of Art

Notre Dame, Indiana
Wightman Memorial Art Gallery

Oakland, California
Oakland Art Gallery

Philadelphia, Pennsylvania
The Pennsylvania Academy of the Fine
Arts
Pennsylvania Museum of Art
The University Museum

Pittsburgh, Pennsylvania
Carnegie Institute Department of Fine
Arts

Pittsfield, Massachusetts
The Berkshire Museum

Providence, Rhode Island
Rhode Island School of Design

Richmond, Virginia
The Richmond Academy of Arts
The Valentine Museum

Rochester, New York
Memorial Art Gallery

Salem, Massachusetts
The Essex Institute

San Antonio, Texas
Witte Memorial Museum

San Marino, California
Henry E. Huntington Library and Art
Gallery

St. Louis, Missouri
City Art Museum of St. Louis

Savannah, Georgia
Telfair Academy of Arts and Sciences

Seattle, Washington
Henry Gallery

Springfield, Massachusetts
The Springfield Museum of Fine Arts

Syracuse, New York
The Syracuse Museum of Fine Arts

Toledo, Ohio
The Toledo Museum of Art

Topeka, Kansas
Washburn College Museum

Trenton, New Jersey
New Jersey State Museum

Washington, D. C.
The Corcoran Gallery of Art
Freer Gallery of Art
Phillips Memorial Gallery
National Gallery of Art

Worcester, Massachusetts
Worcester Art Museum

CONTENTS

I. American Painting 1865-1934

By HOLGER CAHILL

I. AMERICA AFTER THE CIVIL WAR.
EXPATRIATE AND STAY AT HOME — WHISTLER AND HOMER

THE PERIOD between 1865 and 1934 is one year short of the biblical three-score and ten. This period, which saw the rise and development of several generations of important American painters, the emergence of American art from a provincial to a national and cosmopolitan phase, the successive waves of European influence from the romanticism of the 1830's to the equally romantic super-realism and expressionism of today, may be spanned by the life of one man.

At the beginning of the period American art was provincial. It is true, of course, that American art had always been provincial, that is, it was a local dialect of the great language of European art. But with the end of the old portrait school, which had been the glory of the Colonial and early Republican eras, American art, in the decades before the Civil War, sank into an even deeper provincialism. The social classes which had supported the early portrait school had been swamped by the tidal wave of industrialism which carried to power classes with no tradition of art patronage. And to complete the ruin of the portrait school, photography, which had its beginning earlier in the century, had by the 1860's been developed to such a point that it took the place of the painted portrait not only in the affection of the public, but also in the estimation of many painters who did their best to imitate the effects of the camera.

American art was seeking its bearings in an age of profound economic and social change. After the Civil War the momentum of social change was accelerated. The decades immediately following the war have about them the bustling disorder of a vast construction camp. The landed gentry of the East had fallen into decay, or they had joined forces with the leaders of business enterprise. In the South they had been destroyed. The old maritime aristocracy of the Atlantic seaboard had passed. With the decay of these classes went the genteel tradition with its rather mild good taste in the arts. In place of the more cultured older aristocracy, which had never been very large nor very sure of its taste, came the beneficiaries of the booming industrial order—individualists

scrambling for wealth and power, the barons of factory towns, mining towns, coal towns, steel towns, oil towns, the builders of railroads, land grabbers, speculators, carpet-baggers, prospectors, boomers.

A whole nation was "on the make," restless, uprooted, eagerly developing, wasting and destroying the resources of a continent. It was an age of technical achievements, rapid material advances. Inventions multiplied daily. New industries were born almost over night. And from these flowed immense streams of wealth to people who had never had wealth before. It was a time when great fortune attended the ruthless and the pushing—when the rawness of the frontier was matched by the crudeness of the new industrial plutocracy, who cared as little for the more dignified esthetic ideals of the older America as they cared for its more democratic social theory. When they turned to art patronage they showed little discrimination. As Isham * says: "They gratified themselves with fast trotters, diamonds and champagne; they built themselves big and amazingly ugly houses and filled them with furniture whose only excuse was its cost. And with other things they bought pictures. . . ." They bought the largest and the emptiest of the Salon prize-winners, the grandiose landscapes of Bierstadt and Church, the dull portraits of Healy and Huntington, and "monstrous plaster figurines daubed with crazy paint . . . shoddy portrait statues and inane ideal ones . . . ornaments, pictures and sculptures made to gull and to sell."

American art in the decades after the Civil War shares in the qualities which made that extraordinary period of American life, with its crude power, its chaos and its emergent order. At the feet of the great slag mountains of the Gilded Age there were many small plots of green where a rich intellectual and spiritual life was germinating. There were living at the time men and women of extraordinary personal quality. In painting there were Whistler, Homer, Inness, Hunt, La Farge, Eakins, Ryder, Mary Cassatt, Wyant and Homer Martin. And there were others, educators and

* Samuel Isham, *The History of American Painting.*

practical men who were busy extending public education, building museums and art schools, and introducing the study of art into the public schools. There were rich men who gave their art collections to the public. These were genuine contributions and America today is richer for them. Tuckerman, writing in 1867, could say that Chicago, Albany, Buffalo, Philadelphia, Boston and New York had "native ateliers, schools and collections" whose fame "has raised our national character and enhanced our intellectual resources as a people."

In spite of the museums, the art schools and the collectors it was a difficult time for the artists. A sympathetic and discriminating public is a necessary element in the development of a national art. It alone can create an environment in which the artist can function freely and fully. In the decades after the Civil War there was no such public. What public there was found interest only in the kind of art which flattered the pretensions of a careless individualism restlessly engaged with material expansion and the ideal of constantly mounting profits. In such an environment the original artist had little place. He was driven into isolation, forced into the accentuation of personal peculiarities, into bohemianism and defiance. It is true that for the original artist there have been no golden ages, but the era following the Civil War was an age of sounding brass that made bitter harmony for Whistler, Homer, Inness, Hunt, Eakins and Ryder. It was an age of expatriates and solitaries. The question of Henry James, "Is one's only safety, then, in flight?" was answered by many artists in the affirmative. Others remained to accept and to master. The vulgarities of the period and the crude common humanity rising to power were rejected by the sensitive and fastidious Whistler, but they found epic affirmation in the work of Winslow Homer and Thomas Eakins, and an extraordinary sublimation in Albert Pinkham Ryder, though Eakins suffered isolation and neglect, Homer in the end withdrew from humanity to his shack by the sea, and the life of the more sensitive Ryder centered about the one room in which Lao Tze says a man may see the whole universe.

WHISTLER   Tate Gallery, London
THE LITTLE WHITE GIRL

JAMES ABBOTT McNEILL WHISTLER

Whistler, the expatriate, and Homer, the stay-at-home, bring into sharp focus the divergent tendencies of their period. Both were born in Massachusetts in the middle 1830's, when the smoke of factory chimneys was beginning to dim the light of New England transcendentalism and to darken the ideal of a Greek democracy which was the dream of the agrarian South. Whistler was allied by birth to the older American aristocracy. His father and his grandfather had been army men. He himself was destined for a military career, which was cut short by the dislike for hard study which was characteristic of him as a painter. He got some instruction in art from Robert W. Weir at West Point, and studied for two years with Gleyre in Paris. This constituted all his school training. What he learned in Europe he got not so much from his training under Gleyre as from his contact with French painters, Courbet, Manet, Degas, Fantin-Latour, with the English Pre-Raphaelites, and from his studies of Velasquez, the Spanish master, and of Japanese prints.

At the beginning of his career Whistler showed a tendency to follow the French realists in such pictures as *The Thames in Ice* (1859), *Wapping Docks*, and *The White Girl,* (1862) which was shown at the Salon des Refusés in Paris in 1863. By the middle 1860's, under the combined influences of the English Pre-Raphaelites, Velasquez and the Japanese, he had turned from realism to the problems of tone and arrangement. The change is hinted in *The White Girl*, it is stronger in *The Little White Girl,* painted in 1864, and complete in the series of nocturnes, begun in 1865. By this time Whistler's study of Japanese prints had convinced him that the illusion of the third dimension was a vulgar mistake of Western painting, and linear perspective a cheap accomplishment. He had turned from the realistic to the decorative. From this time on we are conscious of an increasing eclecticism in Whistler's work.

Up to the period of the Civil War European critics had considered American art no more than a tasteful résumé of certain European tendencies. Whistler may be considered the heir of this side of the American tradition. The most truly cosmopolitan of American painters, he extends his tasteful résumé of art beyond the boundaries of Europe to the Far East. No painter of the nineteenth century is more cosmopolitan than Whistler. None is more intensely personal. Whistler's cosmopolitanism makes his connection with American art seem rather tenuous, but he does not fit in the French tradition as Mary Cassatt does, and he is far less English than Copley. Whistler's very cosmopolitanism is American. He is the true child of his uprooted time. Like the other expatriates of the nineteenth century, he searched the world for something he did not find in his own country, for the look of the past, for the elusive romantic beauty which is always to be found somewhere else, in another country, in another age. It is the romantic quest, old as the human heart, new as the "lost generation" of the post-war period.

Whistler's quest led him to Europe, but the England in which he finally settled was very much like the America he had left. There were some differences. Taste in England was not altogether dominated by the commercial and industrial plutocracy which dominated it in America. And there was not the same popular indifference to art. Whistler could find in England what his spirit needed, a few loyal friends and patrons, and a host of enemies on whom he could exercise his keen and nimble wit. There was no dearth of enemies. The English academicians of Whistler's time insisted on what they called "finish," a dull mechanical attention to detail very much like that of the Düsseldorfians who were then popular in America. They considered subject matter so important that they would lock their studios while painting exhibition pictures for fear a rival might discover their story. Their ideas about art were rather like those of "the man in the street" in America today. To these ideas Whistler was opposed. For the mechanical "finish" of the academicians he cared not a whit. The human episode in art did not interest him. He believed that art was its own justification; that it needed no social reference, no story, no adventitious trappings from literature or history. He refused to make any concessions to the public, believing that art is a difficult problem which the artist alone can solve, and that the public must be satisfied with his solutions and follow him as best it may.

Whistler's attitude appears extreme today, but it was similar to that of many French painters of the time who were in revolt against the academies. To the English painters and to Ruskin, the most influential art critic of the English-speaking world, it was anathema. The elderly Ruskin, who in his later years turned more and more to social theorizing, could see nothing good in Whistler, the champion of "art for art's sake." The famous Whistler-Ruskin trial brought to a head these antagonisms. Ruskin, possibly forgetting his enthusiasm for Turner, attacked Whistler in a review, accusing him of "ill-educated conceit" which "approached the aspect of wilful imposture." "I have seen and heard much of cockney impudence before now," Mr. Ruskin wrote, "but I never expected to hear a coxcomb ask two hundred guineas for flinging a pot of paint in the public's face." Whistler sued. The trial was a farce which rocked England with Philistine laughter. Whistler won a farthing in damages, and the heavy expense of the trial forced him into bankruptcy.

The picture which moved Ruskin to wrath was *Nocturne in Black and Gold,* exhibited at the Grosvenor Gallery in 1877. The nocturnes illustrate much that is good and all that is bad in Whistler's art. In them and in his later pictures Whistler's composition tends to be two-dimensional, and his delicate harmonies of tone fade toward a misty gray. But in working out his schemes for harmony of tone Whistler was an experimenter far ahead of his time. His rendering of tone is as abstract as that of the Post-Impressionists, but it must be said that his experiments are usually more interesting than his results. The problem with which Whistler struggled was this: often the colors which are beautiful and harmonious in nature seem crude and harsh when set down in pigment, and the painter must devise some consistent method for translating these colors into a harmonious scheme. The problem has been solved in many ways in the history of painting. Whistler's solution was to limit the number of colors which he used, suppressing the contrast between these colors, and also suppressing contrasts of light and shade. This scheme produced the harmony of tone which he desired, but it keyed his pictures down perilously close to the

gray which Delacroix had called the enemy of all painting.

One of Whistler's most successful nocturnes is *Old Battersea Bridge.* It has the harmony of tone brought on by the diming of colors at nightfall or by a misty atmosphere. In pictures such as this one Whistler is the poet of the Thames. The actual scene here counts for little. The handling of tone and form is quite arbitrary. The structure of the bridge has been altered. It is heightened and made much more slender, and its relation to the background has been changed. The artist has transposed quite freely to make the scene more significant and emotionally expressive. No wonder the matter-of-fact jurors at the Whistler-Ruskin trial were mystified!

Not all of Whistler's nocturnes are as successful as *Old Battersea Bridge.* In some of his later pictures form practically disappears and we have an art of hints, of oblique statements which are very difficult to read. Modeling and outline are abandoned for softened and fading contours. Color is grayed until the picture becomes little more than a thin, murky tonal scheme, filled with delicacies and profundities which are not quite real. But there is more in Whistler's art than that. He had a fine decorative sense, a feeling for linear rhythm, for "obscure and lovely arabesques." The feeling for line is evident in Whistler's etchings. His series of etchings on the life of the London waterfront has been greatly admired, and won the praise of so discriminating a critic as Baudelaire. (*Black Lion Wharf*)

Whistler's fine decorative sense and his ability to concentrate upon arrangement and tone without losing his power of sympathetic characterization, his fine

WHISTLER
OLD BATTERSEA BRIDGE

Tate Gallery, London

handling of proportional composition, and his austere selection, in such portraits as *The Artist's Mother*, *Thomas Carlyle* and *Miss Cecily Alexander*, give his work more value than many contemporary critics are willing to admit. Whistler has suffered a temporary eclipse because art today is not much concerned with the problems that interested him. He was too consciously the esthete, and esthetes are in bad repute nowadays. Still he is an important figure in nineteenth century painting. His emphasis on design, in an age of photographic realism, was constructive, and his dictum that good painting leaves out all human interest was a normal reaction against the literary painting of his day.

WINSLOW HOMER

Whistler was an artist of minor chords. He made his art speak in a small refined voice. The art of Winslow Homer is an art of forthright statement as bold and uncompromising as nature herself. Whistler was an eclectic of such wide-ranging interests that the German critic, Meier-Graefe, has called him a case of multiple personality. There was nothing of the eclectic about Winslow Homer. His art has the homespun accent

of American provincial painting. The two men were opposites in almost every way. The one thing they had in common was intense individualism. Homer never bothered about arrangement, never consciously transposed or altered a scene to make it more emotionally expressive, had no method for tone organization other than careful selection of the effects in nature which interested him.

"Do you ever take the liberty, in painting from nature, of modifying the color of any part?" John W. Beatty once asked him.

"Never! Never!" Homer replied. "When I have selected the thing carefully I paint it exactly as it appears." *

Winslow Homer is the most thoroughly American of our painters. Unlike Whistler, he had neither the income with which to escape to Europe nor the will to do so. Except for a few short visits to Europe he lived and worked in America uninterruptedly. Whistler is a product of the art school. Homer was shop-trained, and in this respect his art education did not differ greatly from that of the folk artists of his period. His work comes directly out of the school of popular illustration, and is as peculiarly in the American grain as the prints of Currier & Ives. Homer made sketches as a boy, and when he went into a lithographer's shop at the age of nineteen he already knew something about drawing. After a short experience in Boston as a magazine illustrator he went to New York in 1859, studied for a time in night classes at the National Academy of Design, and took three or four lessons in painting from Frederic Rondel, a French

* W. H. Downes, *The Life and Works of Winslow Homer,* Introduction.

painter living in New York. At the outbreak of the Civil War he went to the front as special correspondent for *Harper's Weekly*.

Homer's pictures from the front and his anecdotal observation of negro life which followed the war brought him a good deal of popular success, not only in America but in Europe. His *Prisoners from the Front* and *The Bright Side* were shown at the Paris International Exhibition of 1867. In these early works Homer gave the Europeans what they expected from American art— the local peculiarity of life in the New World which they found in the writings of Bret Harte and Mark Twain. These peculiarities of American life had already found expression in popular prints and in the works of the earlier genre painters, in John James Audubon, Caleb Bingham and George Catlin, in Eastman Johnson and the Hudson River painters. But Winslow Homer gave it an expression more powerful, more personal and more severely objective. His genre paintings and landscapes have the look and the feel of American earth. They are "baptised in American water."

After the Civil War, Homer devoted himself to magazine illustration and to painting scenes from everyday life. (*Snap the Whip*) The paintings of this period are straightforward, soberly objective, and daring in color. They show that Homer had learned how to avoid the niggling realism of the Hudson River school. He did this not so much by suppression of detail as by sure selection and delimitation of the scene, and an absorption in the subject so intense that he saw only the essentials. But in general the vision in his early

HOMER
SNAP THE WHIP (Wood cut)

Whistler said that nature is rarely right, in fact that she is usually wrong. He said in his writings, and showed in his art, that he cared nothing for subject. Winslow Homer was absorbed in subject. He cared so much about nature that sometimes he waited for years to get the exact effect he needed in a picture, refusing to finish it from memory. He wanted to have the scene before him. At Prout's Neck he used a portable hut which he moved about the shore, so that he could get close to the sea in bad weather and paint the storm on the spot.

This direct way of working is better suited to the watercolorist than to the painter in oils. And it is true that Winslow Homer handled watercolor with an ease and mastery which he never achieved in the oil medium. He is undoubtedly the greatest American watercolorist of the nineteenth century. In oil painting his color is sometimes a little hard and raw, but it must be said that he handled it with unusual boldness and freedom. In this respect he was far ahead of contemporary American "tonalism."

It is in his watercolors that Homer's forceful draughtsmanship and large boldness of construction, his power to suggest mass and movement with the utmost economy of means, and his daring use of

pictures is not keyed up beyond that of the average man. Except for the more daring use of color there is no great leap from these paintings to Eastman Johnson's *Corn Husking* and *Old Kentucky Home.* But in this work Winslow Homer was preparing for the development which carried him away from popular illustration and genre.

The forthright honesty of these earlier pictures, the strength with which the essential structure of figure or landscape is brought out, the simple force of the draughtsmanship, point the way to his later work. Homer's realism is often hard but it is never conventional. Look at the swirls of water in *Hound and Hunter,* the way a blazing fire is suggested in *Camp Fire,* the construction of rocks and water in the foreground of *The Coast of Maine* (all in the Metropolitan Museum, New York) in *Cannon Rock,* or any of the later pictures. This is not realism in any academic sense. Everywhere is breadth, summary but sure handling, and the most unconventional use of color. If Winslow Homer painted only what his eye could see, what an extraordinarily keen and selective eye he had! The fact is, of course, that he was guided in his seeing by a firm conception of what he was trying to do.

In 1876 Homer abandoned illustration and gave himself exclusively to painting. He went to Europe but found little there to interest him. "If a man wants to be a painter," he once said, "he must never look at pictures." It seems probable, however, that Homer knew the watercolors of Turner and Girtin, and that he was not indifferent to the French realists. In 1884 he broke all ties with the outside world, settled at Prout's Neck

on the Maine coast, and devoted most of the remainder of his life to the drama of the sea, the eternal battle of land and water, of man's unbreakable courage against the overwhelming powers of nature. This theme Homer expressed with grand and simple power.

HOMER
CANNON ROCK

HOMER
WINDSTORM—BAHAMAS

Private Collection

HOMER
EIGHT BELLS

Addison Gallery of American Art, Andover, Mass.

color show at their best. During the latter years of his life he spent many winters in Florida and the Antilles, where the brilliant coloring of sky and sea and land gave full scope to his talents. For in color, as in everything else, Winslow Homer was bound by nature. The splendor of the southern seas with their brilliant blues and greens and violets is set down with breadth and mastery. Homer's West Indian watercolors are a thing apart in nineteenth century American painting, and they hold their own today in any modern exhibition. (*Windstorm—Bahamas*)

Winslow Homer had the American sense of fact in high degree. The only American painter who surpasses him in this respect is Thomas Eakins. With Homer the fact is perhaps not so deeply penetrated as with Eakins, but it is handled with more sweep and breadth, and with more sense of drama. Homer was always the illustrator, but the intensity of his absorption in subject, the dramatic force of his presentation, whether in a picture of army camps, of negro life, or of the surf pounding on the rocky coast of Maine, give his work its special quality. He knew how to grasp the essential character of a scene and how to present it with such honesty and compelling force that the spectator realizes, as Isham says, that the scene must have been "thus and not otherwise."

Homer with his broad and dramatic realism and his enthusiasm for the American scene, Whistler with his estheticism, his concern for an art of pure design, are typical representatives of tendencies in American art which have struggled for mastery within our own generation. Today Homer seems the more significant, but there can be no doubt that both men are important in the history of American art. In their separate ways they reacted to American life and expressed the experience of their generation.

II. THREE LANDSCAPE PAINTERS AND A SOLITARY
INNESS, MARTIN, WYANT, RYDER

WINSLOW HOMER remains the most powerful representative of open-air painting in America. This, because he carried out the idea implicit in America's first landscape school, the idea of making pictures out of observation. In this respect he is the heir of the realistic side of the Hudson River tradition, though it is generally considered that the continuators of that tradition are George Inness, Homer D. Martin and Alexander H. Wyant.

The spade work for a native landscape school was done in the first half of the nineteenth century by the Hudson River painters. These men cannot be called great artists. Their work is often thin, poor in color and is usually lost between the insignificances of detail and the sentimentality of the grandiose. But they had a real love for the American landscape, and they responded directly to the inspiration of the country. There is a good deal of charm in Asher Durand's smaller landscapes, for all their plodding literalism, and a real sense of panorama in Cole and Kensett.

The early work of Inness, Martin and Wyant is in the line of the Hudson River panoramas (Inness' *Juniata River* (1856) and *Peace and Plenty* (1865), Martin's *Lake Sanford*, Wyant's *Mohawk Valley*, the last three in the Metropolitan Museum, New York), but in their later work they came to lay less stress upon subject and more upon purely esthetic means for suggesting the mood and the poetry of landscape. Reacting from the analytical realism of the Hudson River painters, they strove for synthesis achieved through harmonious organization of tone, atmospheric treatment and a looser handling, which they learned from the Barbizon painters, the English landscapists, and the early Impressionists.

GEORGE INNESS

The work of George Inness developed steadily in this direction. Inness, like Homer, was largely self-taught. When he began painting, opportunities for art study in America were very meagre. He had a few lessons from Régis Gignoux, a Frenchman who painted Hudson River scenes, but he learned more from engravings and from a study of paintings in European museums. He went to Europe several times. In 1847-48 he spent fifteen months in England and on the continent. In 1871 he went to Europe again and remained four years, mostly in Paris and Rome.

At first Inness tried to make pictures out of direct observation of nature, faithfully depicting the scene as it was before him. This method he soon modified by taking with him on sketching trips engravings of landscapes by the masters, that he might learn from them the breadth for which he was striving. The results of this study and of his contact with European art are evident in such pictures as *Lake Albano* (1869, in Phillips Memorial Gallery, Washington) which has a largeness and unity of conception rare in American landscape painting at the time. A further development of his work took place when he became familiar with the "new natural-

INNESS
LAKE ALBANO

Phillips Memorial Gallery, Washington, D. C.

INNESS
EARLY AUTUMN, MONTCLAIR

ism" of the Barbizon painters. From them he learned a more gracious and intimate landscape, humanized and ordered by man and infused with his sentiments. His interpretation of landscape becomes broader and more lyrical; his brushwork becomes looser, and precise details of form and local tone become of less significance than the general atmospheric scheme.

The transition from the more solidly painted pictures of Inness' earlier years to the later light-filled, impressionistic tone symphonies is illustrated in *The Coming Storm* (1878) in The Albright Art Gallery, Buffalo. *Early Autumn, Montclair* (1888) is a further development in this direction. In paintings like these Inness gets tonal harmony without reducing the intensity of local tones, and a balance between his interest in nature as fact and as mood. In pictures such as *The Home of the Heron* (1893) and *Moonlight on Passamaquoddy Bay* (1893) in the Art Institute of Chicago, both in his all-overish manner, Inness is already lost in the mysticism of his later years. The subject of these pictures is an interplay of delicately balanced tones, blurred in mists of color-charged atmosphere. Their vagueness may be due to the fact that Inness was trying to solve the problem of how a scene may be unified by a glance in which all objects are slightly out of focus as in the blurred image of an over-exposed photograph. It may be due, also, to the fact that in his later years he worked a good deal from memory, feeling that he had his forms "at his finger tips," and that direct observation was no longer necessary.

George Inness was the most cultivated and many-sided of American landscape-ists, but he did not have the terrific drive and single-mindedness of Homer. He was an artist divided against himself. He often said that he "seemed to have two opposing styles—one impetuous and eager, the other classical and elegant." Inness was not quite sure of his intentions, and this accounts for much of the unevenness of his production. His later work is often vague and sometimes flimsy, but at its best it has a certain emotional splendor.

WYANT AND MARTIN

Homer Dodge Martin and Alexander H. Wyant never followed Inness all the way, or rather, their interests were not quite parallel to his. Wyant began his career as a sign painter. At twenty he saw some paintings by Inness and made the journey from Cincinnati to Perth Amboy to ask the advice of the master. In 1865 he went to Europe and got some German training, but he preferred the work of Crome, Constable, Turner and the Barbizon painters. Wyant was an artist of narrow range, a landscape poet, minor but authentic. His favorite subject is a clearing in the forest with a glimpse of sky or sea. (*A Glimpse of the Sea*)

Martin was a painter of moods, but unlike Inness, he never lost sight of the actual. He took naturally to painting and after two weeks' instruction from James Hart is said to have begun turning out pictures. His early work is in the tradition of Cole and Kensett, but shows a better feeling for composition and a color sense which is good though not distinguished. Under the influence of the Barbizon painters he turned from the hard realism of the Hudson River school. After a visit to England in 1876 and several years residence in France beginning in 1881, his style changed radically. He had learned from the early Impressionists how to put "little bits of paint alongside each other to try to make them twinkle." The drawing in these pictures (*View of the Seine* and *Manor House at Criqueboeuf* in the Metropolitan Museum, and *Westchester Hills*) is simpler and more generalized, the paint is laid on heavily, sometimes with the palette knife. The color is higher in key and more cheerful, though Martin's pictures are usually filled with sadness and loneliness. Martin has been called a painter of tragic landscape, but beside the more profoundly thought-out pictures of Ryder his tragedy seems little more than a note of quiet melancholy.

WYANT
GLIMPSE OF THE SEA

The Metropolitan Museum of Art, New York

RYDER—THE SOLITARY

Like Inness, Albert Pinkham Ryder was a painter of emotion and idea, but, unlike Inness, he was sure of his intention. He saw nature as mood completely, and though he never lost his Yankee sense of fact, he never, after his first fumbling efforts, tried to make a picture out of observation. Ryder was born in New Bedford, Massachusetts, when that city was still the greatest whaling port in the world. But in Ryder's boyhood the New England of the seafarers was becoming a thing of the past. Her great ports were falling into decay, one after another, and her sons were turning from the wild embrace of the sea to the factories, the mill towns, and the railroads. It was natural that Ryder, born in the time of New England's maritime decay, painted, not the sea of the mariner, but the brooding, mysterious sea of the poet.

Ryder had some training under William Marshall who had been a pupil of Couture, and he studied for a very short time at the National Academy of Design, but he always had difficulty with what may be called the penmanship of art. There was really no one in Ryder's time who could have taught him the methods he wanted to learn—the method of such late-Renaissance masters as Titian, Veronese and Tintoretto, of building up pictures by overpainting, glazing and scumbling. Ryder had to discover the method for himself. He worked and re-worked his pictures, painfully, for years, laying one coat of paint over another, opaque light over dark,

glazing, painting over the glaze and glazing again. Before he sold the *Oriental Encampment* to a New York dealer he had been working on it for ten years, and before he delivered it he worked on it three more. To a patron who told him that he would have his funeral procession stop by and collect a painting he had commissioned, Ryder replied: "You shan't have it, even then, unless it's finished."

This method of working gives Ryder's

pictures their rich enamel-like quality, but it also explains why so many of them are going to pieces. He once told a painter who visited him that one ruined canvas had been "a fine thing twenty-five years ago, when it was almost finished." All this groping was due partly to Ryder's lack of training, but largely to the fact that he was always trying to reach for something that eluded him. "Have you ever," he once wrote, "seen an inchworm crawl up a leaf or twig, and there clinging to the very end, revolve in the air, feeling for something, to reach something? That's like me. I am trying to find something out there beyond the place on which I have a footing."

Ryder had trouble with technique, but he was right about fundamentals. His design is always large and simple. His pictures are completely thought out in all their parts, constructed with sure intuition, and filled with rhythm and movement. Ryder had a feeling as keen as any Cubist for what is vital and interesting in shapes. He knew how to simplify landscape forms and could use distortion, when it suited his purpose, to make his design stronger. He was concerned with the quality of painted surfaces and used pigment and varnish as materials which are beautiful in themselves.

Ryder was a painter of dreams, and he can make us believe in the reality of dream with purely plastic means. The dream quality in his pictures, their poetic titles, and the verses which he

RYDER
THE FLYING DUTCHMAN

The National Gallery of Art, Washington, D. C.

RYDER
DEATH ON A PALE HORSE

Cleveland Museum of Art

RYDER
TOILERS OF THE SEA

Addison Gallery of American Art, Andover, Mass.

sometimes wrote to go with them, have led some writers to call him a literary painter; but this is an error. Ryder's ideas could be expressed only in the plastic medium, in patterns—the dramatic cloud and moonlight patterns of night skies, (the most interesting skies in American painting), in spots of darkly luminous color glazed and varnished until they glowed like enamel. (*Toilers of the Sea*, Addison Gallery of American Art, Andover, Mass.) He was interested in the relation of shapes and the harmony and balance of beautifully matched tones. To him his *Jonah and the Whale* was not an illustration of the biblical story but "a lovely turmoil of boiling water."

No man could have been more completely opposed to the spirit of his time than Albert Pinkham Ryder. He lived in an age of ostentatious materialism which drove many of America's most talented artists to Europe. But Ryder was so intent on his vision that he was indifferent to the strident world about him. "The artist," he said, "needs but a roof, a crust of bread and his easel, and all the rest God gives him in abundance." Most of his mature life was spent in one room in which his easel was by far the most imposing article of furniture. This room he would not have exchanged for "a palace with less a vision than the old garden with its whispering leafage." He remained to the end of his career the hermit, one of the saints and visionaries of art, set by some divine accident in the midst of America's Gilded Age.

RYDER
THE FOREST OF ARDEN

Dodsworth Estate

FULLER
ROMANY GIRL

Addison Gallery
of American Art,
Andover, Mass.

FULLER AND BLAKELOCK

The story of Ryder's work is one that required the plastic medium, and this is true also of the work of George Fuller and Albert Blakelock. Like Ryder these men were uncertain and laborious craftsmen, but unlike him they were not clear about what they were trying to do. George Fuller began as an itinerant portrait painter and was an associate of the National Academy as early as 1857. The pictures with which his name is now associated were not shown until 1876, after he had been forced to give up painting as a professional career and had spent a number of years in farming. Fuller lacks Ryder's completeness of conception, and is more literary and sentimental. His wistful and shadowy pictures are difficult to read today, but the best of them (*Romany Girl*) have genuine charm and a poetry which results not only from an attitude toward the subject, but also from a method of handling tone and pattern.

If Fuller is more sentimental than Ryder, Blakelock is more obviously deco-

· 17 ·

rative. Blakelock, who was entirely self-taught, was interested in surfaces and was working for tone and for a sort of decorative composition in silhouette, but he was not always successful and his work is rather monotonous. His typical painting is a forest interior in moonlight with tapestry-like tree patterns silhouetted against areas of sky and water. Such pictures as *Brook by Moonlight* (Toledo Museum) and *Moonlight* are interesting in pattern and have a certain muted splendor of tone.

Looking back to the period when Inness, Martin, Wyant, Ryder and Eakins were working, we are struck by the fact that these men had little honor in their own generation. "It was only after a generation of struggle," says Isham, "when second-rate Barbizon pictures had been forced up to prohibitive prices, that it became generally admitted that some Innesses might be as good as some Diazes." Martin lived in straitened circumstances all his life. Eakins found it difficult even to give his pictures away. Without help from his family and from two or three sympathetic collectors and dealers, Ryder would not have been able to keep the one small room which was his studio and home.

The popular and successful painters were those whose vision was close to that of the average man, painters who reflected the spirit of their age at its lowest intensity. Men who expressed that spirit at high intensity, and gave it a distinction and vitality which are the expression not only of a deeper culture but also of a quality of personality, were practically ignored. Not only did these

BLAKELOCK
MOONLIGHT
Collection Horatio S. Rubens, New York

men find it almost impossible to sell their paintings; they also found it difficult to exhibit. The old Academy in New York, which should have been the trial ground of new ideas, was filled with works most of which have ceased to be of importance to American art. There was little space for paintings which did not follow the academic stereotype. It became necessary to organize an opposition to the Academy. This was done by the

Society of American Artists, which opened in 1877 the first American *Salon des Réfusés*. Among the early exhibitors of the Society of American Artists were such men as La Farge, Hunt, Inness, Martin, Ryder and Eakins. During the thirty years of its existence the Society was the most distinguished exhibition group in the country. It was amalgamated with the Academy in 1906 to form the present National Academy of Design.

III. WAVES OF EUROPEAN INFLUENCE — HUNT, LA FARGE, DUVENECK, CHASE. PORTRAIT PAINTERS, FASHIONABLE AND UNFASHIONABLE — EAKINS, SARGENT

IN THE decades after the Civil War American art was going through a period of rapid change and development. The influence of Europe upon American painting and sculpture became increasingly insistent. Communication and travel between the two continents was made easier. Improvements in printing and engraving methods increased the number of publications which brought European art and ideas before the American public. The cultural lag, which had made an eighteenth century American a seventeenth century European, was shortened to less than a generation. The Barbizon influence was a strong current in American art by the 1870's,

and the work of the French Impressionists was familiar here by the 1890's. Artists in increasing number found it possible to travel and study abroad.

By the 1870's many well-trained technicians were returning from Paris and Munich bringing with them the cosmopolitanism of European ateliers. There were among these men many able and some brilliant artists. In the middle 1870's they were making their power felt in America, and they, together with Whistler and Homer, had convinced Europe that American art was no longer merely a tasteful but rather tepid rewarming of European art, but an independent growth worthy of respect.

American artists had had no section to themselves at the Paris world exhibition of 1855. In 1867 they had a small gallery, and by 1878 the American section was respectable both in numbers and in quality. More important still, the men of the 1870's were founding new art schools in this country or vitalizing old ones. The American artists of the sixties and seventies were either self-taught or they had to go to Europe for the right kind of training. The young painters who came along in the seventies, eighties and nineties could choose among a number of excellent teachers at home. By the close of the century art teaching in America had been revolutionized. Men like John Sloan, Arthur B. Davies, George Bellows, Jerome Myers, Glenn Coleman and Charles Sheeler had no difficulty getting a sound art education in this country.

The most important of the artists who brought the culture of Europe to America in the third quarter of the nineteenth century are William Morris Hunt, John La Farge, Frank Duveneck and William Merritt Chase. The earliest of these is Hunt. With John La Farge and George Inness, he is responsible for the predominance of the French influence in this country. From the third quarter of the nineteenth century American artists and collectors turned increasingly to France, the great animator of international art during the period which we are discussing. Save for the interlude of Munich, with its cult of technique based on direct drawing with the brush, the French influence has been dominant.

WILLIAM MORRIS HUNT

On the whole, this influence has been beneficial. At the time William Morris Hunt returned from France and settled in New England in the late fifties, it was very necessary for the health of American art. Hunt is the first American figure painter of his time to break with the laborious, dull, smooth methods of the Düsseldorfians. After a short period of study at Düsseldorf he entered the studio of Couture in Paris where he remained for five years. The most important influence in his life, however, is that of the Barbizon painters, Diaz and Millet. Hunt, like Inness, saw nature as mood. He believed that "when you paint what you see you paint an object. When you paint what you feel you paint a poem." Hunt was one of the best por-

LA FARGE
THE ASCENSION
Church of the Ascension, New York

trait painters in this country in the 1860's and 1870's, and some of his small landscapes have a good deal of charm. Because of his ill-fated decorations for the capitol at Albany he will always be remembered as a pioneer of American mural painting. His better known pictures, such as *The Bathers* in the Metropolitan Museum, while interesting, give the impression that he was more the man of culture than the artist. "What have you to say with it?" Millet asked him when he saw what he had learned in the studio of Couture. Though he spent most of his life in this country, Hunt was to the end a restless, romantic spirit, ill at ease in the fiercely practical Amer-

ican world. "In another country," he said, "I might have been a painter." But Millet's question remains.

JOHN LA FARGE

Hunt's greatest contribution was in his influence upon collectors and artists, especially upon John La Farge. The two men met in the studio of Couture in Paris where both were students. Later La Farge studied with Hunt at Newport. Like Hunt, La Farge was a man of broad culture. Both men were friends of Henry and William James, of Henry Adams and of the architect, H. H. Richardson. Adams said of La Farge that "of all his friends La Farge alone owned a mind complex enough to contrast against the commonplaces of American uniformity."

La Farge was descended from a French family which came here from the West Indies. Among his immediate ancestors were a number of amateurs of painting, and these guided his first steps in art. Through other relatives who were in the thick of things in Paris he came into contact with the intellectual movements which were then stirring Europe. He studied for a time with Couture, copied old masters all over Europe, came into contact with the Pre-Raphaelites, looked at Japanese prints, and read Chevreul on glass and on color. Though his training was rather desultory he was a learned painter, an eclectic of remarkable range who painted portraits, landscapes and murals, invented opaline glass, and wrote and lectured on paint-

HUNT
LANDSCAPE
The Metropolitan Museum of Art, New York

ing and decorative art. La Farge was enamored of the grand style of the Italian Renaissance in a period when the trend in art was all toward naturalism. He was concerned with tone organization and the effect of light on local color, and his *Paradise Valley, Newport,* a landscape painted in the sixties, anticipated to some extent the discoveries of the Impressionists. But La Farge was much more traditionalist than innovator, except in the making of stained glass. He knew the arts of Europe and of the Far East, and founded upon the great European tradition a personal style that is thoughtful, decorative and refined, but lacking in power. His most important contribution was in the field of mural painting. The work he did for Trinity Church in Boston and for

the Church of the Ascension, New York, set a standard for mural art which has not been surpassed in this country. It is for his murals chiefly, for his work in stained glass, and for his insistence that painters go back to the sources of tradition in the work of the masters, that John La Farge will be remembered.

FRANK DUVENECK

Since the middle of the nineteenth century the French have exerted the greatest influence on American art, but for a time in the seventies Munich overshadowed Paris because of the work and teaching of Frank Duveneck and William Merritt Chase. The basis of art teaching in France was drawing. The French teachers took to heart the saying

of Ingres that "drawing is the probity of art." They made their students draw carefully and accurately from the nude model, and, except for Carolus Duran, the teacher of Sargent, paid little attention to brushwork. In Munich the students learned first of all how to manipulate paint. They drew directly with a heavily loaded brush, defining planes and masses in bold strokes. The Munich method gave an appearance of great technical skill, of breadth and dash. When the works of Frank Duveneck were shown at the Boston Art Club in 1875 they created a sensation. Duveneck on the whole is the soundest of the Munich men, though excellent work in the Munich manner was done by J. Frank Currier. But Currier's talent never found complete expression, and since he lived abroad for thirty years his work is little known in this country.

Duveneck had traveled about the Middle West as assistant to a decorator of churches before he went to Europe. He studied in Munich with Diez and admired the works of Velasquez and of the Flemish and Dutch masters, especially Hals and Rembrandt. He lived and taught in Munich for many years and was looked up to as a master by his American pupils. Duveneck's portraits show a keen eye for the surface aspects of character (*Whistling Boy*). They have the adroit workmanship of Munich, with its bituminous backgrounds and dark shadows which give his pictures the superficial look of time-darkened old masters. He was an excellent etcher, technically somewhat akin to Whistler. In 1889, after the death of his wife, Duveneck went to Cincinnati and spent the rest of his life there in teaching, a field in which he was important. The America of his day needed his insistence on technique.

WILLIAM MERRITT CHASE

Chase, like Duveneck, is important as a teacher. After a short period of study in the Middle West and at the National Academy of Design, Chase went to Munich where he studied under Wagner and Piloty. His early pictures have the dash and bravura at which Munich aimed, its slashing brushwork and dark shadows. Later, Chase came under the influence of the French and abandoned to some extent his earlier methods. But he remained to the end the leading American apostle of the heavily loaded brush. He had a somewhat better color sense than Duveneck, and greater luminosity which he got from the Impressionists. An able painter, but not profound, Chase left a considerable body of work, portraits, landscapes, genre and

DUVENECK
WHISTLING BOY

The Cincinnati Art Museum

still life, of varying quality (*Head of a Man.*) He was for many years a popular teacher at the Art Students' League and at the Chase School which he founded. He emphasized "good painting," brushwork instead of drawing, as the foundation of a picture, and delight in the painter's medium for its own sake.

THAYER AND DEWING

With these men may be grouped the Paris-trained Abbott Handerson Thayer and Thomas Wilmer Dewing, who catered to American sentiment in their idealized visions of woman. Thayer, a pupil of Gérôme, was the more robust of the two, and paid his homage to the eternal woman in figures of athletic and winged virgins. His best work is in his later portraits. (*Woman in Green Velvet*) Dewing, a pupil of Boulanger and Lefebvre, is master of a mellifluous and frail tonalism in which the contours of infinitely refined ladies fade into equally refined mists of color (*The Recitation*).

ALFRED Q. COLLINS

A better painter than Thayer or Dewing, but little known, is Alfred Q. Collins. His work is characterized by completeness of vision, patient searching of form, and an absence of facile formulas. Collins' portraits show a good deal of insight into character, as well as simplicity and charm. Especially pleasing in its sensitive modelling and fine handling of color is his *The Artist's Wife* in the Metropolitan Museum.

PORTRAIT PAINTERS, FASHIONABLE AND UNFASHIONABLE— EAKINS, SARGENT

The influence of European methods which became so insistent in the middle seventies was not an unmixed blessing for American art. It was good when the artist took it as the starting point of his education and worked through it to something personal. "Only when you have denied me will I return to you," Zarathustra said to his pupils. Most American cosmopolitans of the seventies and eighties never got away from their studio training. The lure of technique was too strong for them, and technique for technique's sake has never produced great art. One feels in their work the dull weight of pedantry—the pedantry of the provincial bedazzled with the brilliance he has acquired in the capitals of the great world.

THOMAS EAKINS

The good and the bad in European training in the latter half of the nine-

CHASE
HEAD OF A MAN

teenth century is illustrated in the careers of Thomas Eakins and John Singer Sargent. Sargent remained to the end the brilliant pupil, a kind of super Carolus Duran. Eakins, who studied with Gérôme and Bonnat, made what he took from his teachers into something peculiarly his own. Though his interests were not as wide-ranging as those of Whistler and La Farge he was as thoroughly schooled in the European tradition as either of these men. After five years' study at the Pennsylvania Academy of the Fine Arts, during which time he laid the foundation for his solid understanding of anatomy by taking a regular physician's course in the subject at Jefferson Medical College, Eakins went abroad in 1866. He spent a little over two years in the studio of Gérôme; stud-

ied a short time with Bonnat and with the sculptor Dumont. In 1869 he went to Spain where he admired particularly the work of Ribera and Velasquez.

Before he saw the work of Velasquez, Eakins' method of painting was that of his teacher, Gérôme. He would make an accurate drawing, carefully shaded, and then cover it with paint, part by part. There was no teaching of painting as such in the studio of Gérôme, no training in that cuisine of art which was stressed at Munich. There was no copying of the works of the masters. When Eakins had studied Velasquez he abandoned the method of Gérôme, and developed, independently, a more painter-like technique. He began drawing directly with the brush, blocking in

DEWING
THE RECITATION
The Detroit Institute of Arts

the masses at once, noting the main constructional planes, establishing the right relation of tone, and then built up the picture with successive applications of paint. This method is not unlike that of Sargent and the Munich men. But Eakins, who had been trained in a school of draughtsmen, took seriously the dictum of Ingres that drawing is the probity of art, and he made innumerable sketches and studies of his subjects before he began to paint.

After a few months in Spain, Eakins returned to his native Philadelphia in 1870. He taught for a time at the Pennsylvania Academy until his emphasis upon anatomy shocked the Victorian prudery of the Academy officials. His whole method was based upon anatomy. He worked like a scientist, resumed his studies at Jefferson Medical College, did a lot of dissection, and made quantities of anatomical casts. All this research gave him a profound knowledge of the structure of the human figure. This knowledge and his own love of thoroughness and method Eakins passed on to his pupils at the Pennsylvania Academy, at his own short-lived school in Philadelphia, and at the National Academy of Design in New York. Undoubtedly the soundest American art teacher of his period, he was limited by lack of opportunity. His greatest influence is in the work of members of the Henri group who got his teaching not

THAYER   Addison Gallery of American Art, Andover, Mass.
WOMAN IN GREEN VELVET

COLLINS
THE ARTIST'S WIFE
The Metropolitan Museum of Art, New York

from Eakins himself but from his assistant and follower, Thomas Anshutz.

During his early years in Philadelphia, Eakins painted many episodes from contemporary life, domestic scenes, scenes of boating, fishing, hunting and the prize ring. It is the world of plain men and women painted with a sober, searching realism and a mastery of means which have not been surpassed in this country. By the middle seventies he had produced such pictures as *The Pair-Oared Shell* (Pennsylvania Museum), *The Biglen Brothers Turning the Stake* (Cleveland Museum of Art) and *The Chess Players* (Metropolitan Museum), which rank him as the greatest of American genre painters, with the single exception of Winslow Homer. In 1875 he painted *The Gross Clinic,* the masterpiece of his early period. This painting, dominated by the powerful portrait of Dr. Gross, is one of the very best of Eakins' large compositions. It is lifted out of the plane of genre by its realistic probity, its strength of characterization and its dramatic force.

Toward the middle eighties Eakins devoted himself more and more to portraiture, painting pictures of his family and his friends. He had few commissions. Most of these portraits were painted purely for the love of it. Unlike Sargent he had no quick, brilliant methods. He worked slowly and painstakingly, setting down with searching and powerful objectivity the facts of form and character. "That's the way it is," he would say. But most of his sitters could not see it Eakins' way. His unsparing revelation was distasteful to them. Their feelings were expressed by

the painter, Edwin A. Abbey, when he explained why he would not sit for Eakins. "Because he would bring out all the traits of my character that I have been trying to hide from the public for years." One of the few who liked his portrait by Eakins was Walt Whitman. "Eakins' picture grows on you," he said. "It is not all seen at once. It dawns on you only gradually . . . the more I get to realize it the profounder seems its insight." . . . "Eakins is not a painter, he is a force." But other sitters did not care for this profound insight. They would leave their portraits in Eakins' studio, hide them away or destroy them. One fashionable lady, dismayed by Eakins' portrait of her, asked if her maid might not complete the sittings! There was in truth something dismaying about Eakins' unbending sense of fact.

This sense of fact is the strength of Eakins, and it is also his weakness. In his best work the fact has been looked at so steadily and penetrated so deeply that pure form, a solid realistic form, is achieved in spite of casualness in composition. Eakins was not a good composer. The weakness in his work is unassimilated fact, unassimilated, that is, to the needs of design. He concentrated so intensely upon the central fact that he frequently forgot about the background, leaving it empty or unsatisfactorily related, so that we have a powerfully realized head or figure lost in a barren stretch of canvas. Eakins is at his best in figure compositions like *The Pathetic Song* where a simple, traditional pyramid design is used with excellent effect. In single figures or portraits, especially in the construction of the head, he attains a truth and solidity of realization which is monumental.

Searching observation, profound knowledge of realistic form, uncompromising objectivity, deep sincerity and detestation of shallow prettiness and flourish—these are the qualities of the art of Thomas Eakins. He painted the America of the last quarter of the nineteenth century and his paintings have in them the rugged individualistic solidity, the staid dusky color, and something of the drabness of the period. As in the novels of Theodore Dreiser, form and technique are in harmony with subject. Eakins' iron sense of fact, his localism, his response to the average environment of his time, make him one of the most vital and powerful contributors to the American realistic tradition. He was the soundest and most distinguished figure painter of his generation, and one of the most unpopular. During his later years he worked in increasing obscurity and isolation. That his generation did not beat a path to his door, but followed instead the tinselled procession of Sargent is not astonishing. Eakins' work has the strength and the cruelty of truth. Sargent's has the cruelty of emptiness. And emptiness is always more palatable than truth.

JOHN SINGER SARGENT

John Singer Sargent, most fashionable portrait painter of his generation, was born of American parents in Florence. As a boy he came into contact with that European culture which American expatriates were trying so hard to assimilate. After some study at the Academy in Florence, he entered the studio of Carolus Duran in Paris in 1874. His training was exactly the opposite of Eakins'. There was no painstaking con-

centration on drawing. The student was taught how to approximate the main masses of a composition over the whole surface of a canvas, using a flat brush loaded with paint, drawing, modeling and painting all at one stroke. The technique, as taught by Duran and practiced by Sargent, was a popularization of methods which Manet had derived from certain of the later pictures of Velasquez and Frans Hals. It was the method of the camera eye, of quick surface observation, vivid impressions of the look of things as the eye sees them, without thought or interpretation, set down with quick, flashing brushwork. This method Sargent mastered with ease. It was said that as a student he could

make one brush stroke count for five and cover a canvas with paint before the other students were well started. He attracted a great deal of attention while he was still in Duran's studio and before he was twenty was already considered a brilliant portrait painter. In 1879 he went to Spain where he studied Velasquez and produced such pictures as *El Jaleo* (Gardner Museum, Boston) in which his ability to set down quickly and accurately the momentary look of a scene shows at its best.

By 1881 Sargent had turned definitely to portraiture. From the beginning he had more commissions than he could fill. And this is practically his life story. Sargent added nothing, save his own

extraordinary facility, to the method of his master. He went from country to country, painting fashionable people fashionably, living more in London than anywhere else, visiting America occasionally. His technical dexterity made it easy for the great ones of the world to sit for him. With a dash and a brilliance which astonished and delighted his fashionable patrons he transferred to canvas, in one or two sittings, all the momentary glitter of their mundane elegance. All is surface sparkle and brilliance, the veracity of the moment, the movement of the brush, the ingratiating surfaces of pigment. Some of his earlier portraits, such as that of *Mrs. Charles Gifford Dyer* (1880, Chicago Art Institute), show a sympathetic understanding of character and a sound use of his brilliant technique. In the more ambitious later portraits, for instance *The Wyndham Sisters*, the loose conception of the whole and the flimsy handling in passages which did not interest the painter give an effect of ostentatious emptiness which is distressing. Almost everything here has been sacrificed to the sentimentality of elegance.

The contemporary view of Sargent was that he was searching, detached and sometimes cruel in his analysis of character. The fact appears to be that Sargent was a good reader of commonplaces, but of any profound understanding of character he had not a trace. He had nothing of the bitter, searching truth of Eakins. His method, of course, did not call for it. He expressed very clearly the petty ideals of his period, though he himself was not aware of their pettiness. There is very little distinction of design or even of pattern in most of his canvases. His arrangements have something of the charm of the accidental, especially in the single portraits where the problem of placing on the canvas is not very difficult. Sargent remained to the end simply an eye and a hand. Late in life he turned in boredom from his fashionable portraits to outdoor painting, but he was bound to his method. His fatal facility had undone him. "Art must be incorruptible," said the master of Aix. "It cannot be incorruptible part of the time." Sargent was the most fashionable portrait painter of his time. But time has not respected his fashionable reputation.

EAKINS
THE GROSS CLINIC

The Metropolitan Museum of Art, New York

SARGENT
THE WYNDHAM SISTERS

Corcoran Gallery of Art, Washington, D. C.

EAKINS
THE PATHETIC SONG

IF THE various and conflicting tendencies in American art during the nineteenth century could be summarized in a phrase, that phrase would be "back to nature." The Hudson River painters had tried to make pictures out of their observation of American landscape—with them it is always the nature of observed fact, of sentiment or of grandeur. In the work of Inness, Martin and Wyant it is the nature of mood and intimacy, seen broadly. The Impressionists carried to its logical conclusion the naturalistic research of the nineteenth century. The word impressionism covers a wide territory in painting, and the specific application of impressionist method differs with each painter. In its original sense its meaning is quite obvious, the conveying of quick and vivid impressions of scene or character, the recording of what the eye can take in at a glance. One might say that impressionism is the method of the half-closed eye, in which all objects are thrown slightly out of focus, and fused in a single plane.

A convenient point of departure for nineteenth century Impressionism is the work of Manet, whose saying, "The principal person in the picture is the light," may be taken as the central text of later Impressionist theory. Manet saw nature as a collection of areas differing in color and in the amount of light which they receive. He modeled with flat patches of tone, in a chiaroscuro of color instead of the traditional chiaroscuro of light and shade, and this method, which was carried further by the later Impressionists, culminated in the work of Cézanne. In this view of nature, mass is of more importance than line, since, as Manet said, "there are no lines in nature," only areas of tone defined by contrast at their

HASSAM
ALLIES' DAY, FIFTH AVENUE

Glenn Ford McKinney Estate

edges. Sculptural modeling yields to softened contours and a flattened pattern, as in the work of Whistler.

Impressionism, spelled with a capital "I," was a name given by hostile critics to the work of a group of painters who carried further the naturalistic research of Manet. The pioneers of the group are the Frenchmen Claude Monet and Camille Pissarro and the Englishman Alfred Sisley. These artists cleared the palette of the dark colors used by earlier painters, including Manet, getting the opposition of light and shadow in contrasts of complementary colors without the use of strong darks. They employed, so far as possible, the colors of the solar spectrum, but this spectral palette of the Impressionists was neither so important nor so widely used as is commonly imagined. More important was the fact that the colors were not mixed on the palette but, as Homer Martin put it, were laid on in "little bits of paint alongside each other to try to make them

ROBINSON
SPRING IN GIVERNY

The Milch Galleries, New York

twinkle." This method of divided color was an attempt to approximate with the duller hues of pigment the brilliance of outdoor sunlight. The method had been foreseen to some extent in the Renaissance. It was anticipated by Delacroix and Manet, and formulated as a theory by Monet and Pissarro after they had seen the paintings of the Englishmen Turner and Constable and the Dutchman Jongkind. The experiments of scientists, who discovered that pure colors laid on the canvas side by side in small patches and mixed at a certain distance by the eye are more luminous than the same colors mixed on the palette, were also important in the formulation of Impressionist theory.

The Impressionists painted in a high key, using pure colors at their highest intensity mixed only with adjacent colors or with white. Their pictures were at the farthest possible extreme from the bituminous murk of the Munich painters. "Painting," said Degas, "was first coffee, then coffee with milk, then all milk." Impressionism was the all-milk stage of painting. The subject of the Impressionists was light, and since light changes very quickly their method reduced painting to a record of the most fleeting effects. Classic examples of this are the haystacks which Claude Monet painted at various hours of the day to show how they changed with the changing light. The critics of Impressionism complained that its votaries banished mind from art, reducing the painter to nothing but an eye— "but what an eye!" as Cézanne said of Monet.

A number of American painters whose names are well known to gallery-goers today felt the influence of Impressionism: John H. Twachtman, J. Alden Weir, Maurice Prendergast, Childe Hassam, Ernest Lawson, William J. Glackens, Frederick C. Frieseke, Allen Tucker and Mary Cassatt, though Cassatt is more closely related to Manet and Degas. Several of these painters were members of "The Ten," a group of the most advanced artists of the 1890's who exhibited together.

The earliest American Impressionist was Theodore Robinson, a painter who died before he had reached the full maturity of his powers. He was a pupil of Gérôme and Carolus Duran, and worked with Monet at Giverney. Robinson approached the problem of painting light with considerable skill and was competent in his handling of the figure, but he is rather arid, and since Impressionism is not so well suited to figure painting as to landscape, he modified its method of discontinuity in applying color as his style matured.

A more typical Impressionist is Childe Hassam (*Allies' Day, Fifth Avenue*). His color has warmth and considerable brilliance and he is in many ways a robust outdoor painter, but his construction is less firm than Weir's or Twachtman's, and as a figure painter he cannot be compared with Mary Cassatt.

J. Alden Weir, like Eakins, was a pupil of Gérôme. He felt strongly the influence of Bastien Le Page and the *Plein-airists* who tried to see nature with eyes cleared of the accumulation of tradition and to paint its varying light and shadow and enveloping atmosphere. From *Plein-airism* to Impressionism is only a step, but it was a step which most academicians of Weir's time were unwilling to take. Weir was a vigorous painter of landscapes and figures and too good a draughtsman to sacrifice contour and pattern to light. He has a feeling for harmonies of silvery tones, the gray and brown open-air coloring of Bastien Le Page (*The Donkey Ride*). He was also a good etcher.

Maurice Prendergast was one of the first American painters to make a study of the works of Cézanne. He had a distinctively personal style, a sort of broadly decorative Impressionism in which form is handled with summariness and freedom. His paintings are like color-tapestries built up with patches of pure color (*The Swans*). William J. Glackens, trained as a newspaper illustrator, has a keen eye for the character and movement of a scene (*Chez*

WEIR
THE DONKEY RIDE

J. Alden Weir Estate

PRENDERGAST
THE SWANS

Phillips Memorial Gallery, Washington, D. C.

LAWSON
CENTRAL PARK, WINTER

Collection F. Newlin Price, New York

GLACKENS
CHEZ MOUQUIN

The Art Institute of Chicag

Mouquin). He developed from an early dark manner, which, like that of Henri, is close to the dark period of Manet, to a luminous and exaggerated red-blond warmth like that of the later paintings of Renoir. Ernest Lawson is a lyrical landscape painter whose earlier Impressionism has been considerably modified in the past few years. He is a good composer with a decorative bent, and is close to Twachtman who influenced his early years (*Central Park, Winter*).

JOHN H. TWACHTMAN

John H. Twachtman studied in Munich under Duveneck and Löfftz, and in Paris under Boulanger and Lefebvre, but his contact with the Impressionist movement turned him away from the virtuosity and the coffee color of Munich. Twachtman was the first teacher to bring the theories and methods of Impressionism before art students in this country, and his teaching was important in determining the direction of the younger painters at the turn of the century. His pictures at first glance look like delicate blond mists of color. On closer inspection they are seen to be excellently composed, with a structural integrity and carrying power beyond those of many more obviously "strong" pictures. Twachtman was a keen observer with an eye for the variations and contrasts of tone and he handled the relation of high-keyed tones in diffused light with great subtlety. There is a very beautiful luminosity in his best landscapes, especially the snow scenes, achieved through the use of white. It has been pointed out that the high key and the brilliant and harmonious light in Impressionist pictures depends much more on the use of white mixed with colors of high intensity than it does upon the spectral palette or the divided touch. This may be verified by a study of such pictures as Monet's *Rouen Cathedral,* in the Metropolitan Museum, or any of Twachtman's snow scenes. Twachtman was a fine draughtsman. His feeling for linear rhythm is evident in his etchings. He was one of the most delicately sensitive of American Impressionists, and one of the strongest (*Hemlock Pool*).

MARY CASSATT

Mary Cassatt is the one American Impressionist who disputes the supremacy of Twachtman. It is true, of course, that she is not an Impressionist of the same type. Her work is closer to that of Degas and the later work of Manet. Mary Cassatt is one of the sturdiest and most independent spirits in the history

TWACHTMAN
HEMLOCK POOL

Addison Gallery of American Art, Andover, Mass.

of American painting. She was born in Pittsburgh, Pa., of an old American family of French and Scotch ancestry. After a period of study at the Pennsylvania Academy of the Fine Arts she went to Paris. She spent some time in the atelier of Chaplin, one of the fashionable painters of the period, but most of her study was done in museums. In Italy she studied Correggio and in Spain, Velasquez. (Both of these artists may be considered among the ancestors of Impressionism.) In the Prado she saw the work of Rubens and later went to Antwerp to make a more thorough study of the works of the Flemish master. From 1874 until her death in 1927 Mary Cassatt lived in or near Paris. Degas noticed one of her pictures in the Salon of 1874, the head of a young girl painted under the influence of Rubens. "That is genuine," he said. "There is one who sees as I do." In 1877 Degas invited

her to show with the Impressionist group. "Already," she says, "I had recognized who were my true masters. I admired Manet, Courbet, Degas. I hated conventional art. Now I began to live."

Mary Cassatt's work developed under the influence of Manet and Degas, but she studied with neither. Like the Impressionists she was concerned with problems of light, but she did not use the divided touch or the spectral palette, and was an Impressionist only in the high key and luminosity of her color. She had something of Eakins' probity of vision and was an able technician in several mediums, oil, watercolor, pastel and etching. Her color prints are among the very best things of their kind produced in her generation (*The Bath*). She was an excellent draughtsman, with a feeling for linear design which was enhanced by her admiration for the work of Degas and by her study of Japanese art. Degas once, looking at a picture of hers, denied that a woman could draw so well. Her modeling is never elaborate. The form is set down simply, the composition unpretentious but sound, the masses placed so as to form pleasing arrangements. Her favorite subjects are the young girl and the mother and child (*Girl Combing Her Hair*) and while she handles them with a great deal of sentiment there is not a trace of sentimentality. Her work is robust and charming, filled with honest, healthy sentiment. "Mary Cassatt has much charm," said Gauguin, seeing her work in the exhibition of 1879. "But she has more force."

Mary Cassatt is more thoroughly in the French tradition than any other American painter. She fits into it seemingly without effort. And she is not a mere imitator, for she has assimilated the tradition in its depth and context as well as in its technique. Of the American expatriates of the nineteenth century, she and Henry James, the novelist, are the only ones who found solid footing in Europe. Mary Cassatt was the perfect Henry James American lady, rich, cultured, filled with infinite reticences and profundities, but strong and healthy in her outlook. She was far more European than Whistler or Sargent, but, as she herself maintained to the last, she was a thorough American. She was, on the whole, a painter of more solid achievement than any other member of the American Impressionist group. And by the testimony of European critics and artists, she is one of the few American painters of the nineteenth century whom Europe unreservedly admires. Like William Morris Hunt and Arthur B. Davies, she was one of the few paint-

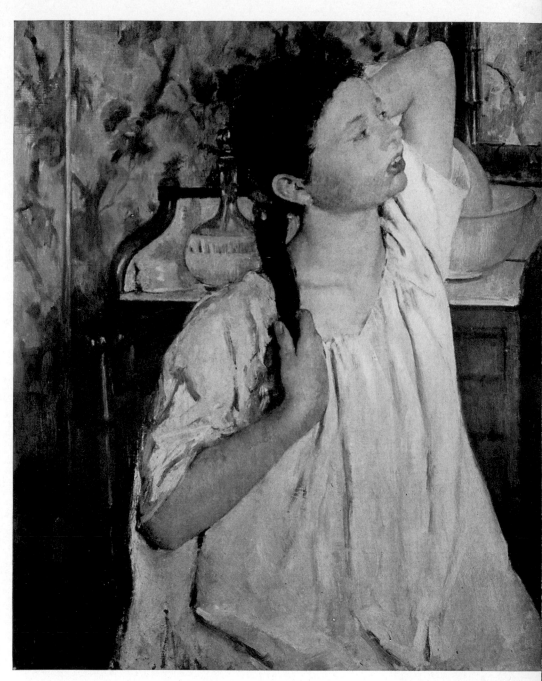

CASSATT Chester Dale Collection
GIRL COMBING HER HAIR

ers with excellent taste in selecting the work of other artists and she helped form some of the best collections in America, particularly the fine Havemeyer collection now at the Metropolitan Museum.

CASSATT Collection Durand-Ruel, Inc.
THE BATH (Color-etching)

THE AMERICAN SCENE—REPORTERS IN INDEPENDENCE— HENRI, DAVIES, SLOAN, LUKS, BELLOWS, COLEMAN

A WHOLE generation of American painters felt the stimulating force of Impressionism, and a much diluted brand of it is still the stock-in-trade of many academic landscape painters. At the close of the century the tag ends of the Düsseldorf and the Barbizon movements, *Plein-airism* and whatnot still echoed in the academies. The portraits of Sargent were extolled as the best since Reynolds. Most painters in this country were devotees of the hard, tight naturalism which they had learned in the studios of Paris or of the cult of the slashing stroke which they had learned in Munich.

In this heavy mass Impressionism was a leaven, not only the luminist Impressionism of Monet, but also the earlier Impressionism of Manet, which served as a point of departure for the Henri group. The original members of this group were Robert Henri, John Sloan, George Luks, William J. Glackens and Everett Shinn. With the exception of Henri, the members of the group had been newspaper illustrators. In the nineteenth century illustration was the school of many American painters. Winslow Homer came out of magazine illustration. Sloan, Luks, Glackens and a host of others got much of their training on newspapers in a day when modern methods of photo-engraving had not been perfected and the pictorial reporter was a standard feature of the daily press. This training gave them experience in depicting scenes from everyday life. One of the things these newspaper-trained artists believed in was the relevance of art to life, to the life of the man in the street. They were interested in social and political ideas, in the writings of Edward Bellamy and Henry George, the optimistic Americanism of Walt Whitman, the humanitarianism of Tolstoy, the economic and historical theories of Karl Marx, in the labor movement, in the whole complex of late nineteenth century idealism which ranged from old-fashioned liberalism to socialism and communism.

These painters, artists of the passing show of city streets, did a great deal to free American art from its shallow estheticism, its Victorian sentimentality and its cult of insipid prettiness. They were fortified in this effort by the example of Eakins and Manet, both of whom preferred the beauty of character to the sugary "beauty" which was the ideal of academicians the world over. On the technical side they emphasized the methods of the painters who had influenced Manet, the great observers of life and character, Velasquez, Goya and Hals. In retrospect their program seems moderate enough, but when they first showed as a group in New York in 1908 they were anathematized as "The Ashcan School" and "The Revolutionary Black Gang."

About the turn of the century most of the members of the Philadelphia group had moved to New York where they were joined by Arthur B. Davies, Ernest Lawson and Maurice Prendergast. They formed an exhibition group known as "The Eight." The group represented a diversity of aims and ideas, and was held together mainly by its opposition to academism. Davies was a romanticist. Prendergast, Lawson and Glackens have been considered with the Impressionists. Shinn has become an illustrator. Henri was a spirited technician who had studied at the *Ecole des Beaux Arts* and the Julian Academy in Paris. Henri was not so different in his technical approach from Chase and Sargent. His difference

was that his vision was more honest, and he cared more about life than he did about paint. Like Sargent he had a deft, flashing technique, broad fluent brushwork, raciness, energy and occasional thinness. His earlier manner, typified by such pictures as *Young Woman in Black,* is probably his best.

It was as a teacher that Henri had his greatest importance. He brought a new note into the American art school. With teachers like Chase and Duveneck technique was the thing, "good painting," the quality of the painted surface. These things counted with Henri, too. He was as masterly a technician as either of these men. But what Henri stressed above everything was the spirit of art, the depth and sincerity of its vision of life. Technique was nothing unless it served as a vehicle for the expression of life. Henri was interested in how a thing was done, but his first question was always "'What have you to say with it?" He loved life and he loved people. His insistence that art must be relevant to the world in which the artist lives was important in the development of a whole generation of American painters, especially such men as George Bellows. He wanted his pupils to paint great pictures, and he filled them with his own fine enthusiasm. Henri was hospitable to new ideas, even when they were opposed to his own. He was one of the few older men who welcomed the Armory Show, which to Chase and many other painters seemed the end of art.

Although Arthur B. Davies showed with "The Eight" he had no real connection with the group except that he shared their opposition to academism and their adventurous interest in new ideas. The Henri group accepted life on its own terms and rejected all forms of prettiness or mere charm. Davies withdrew from life into a world of his own. The object of all his pictures is charm, the charm of young bodies rendered with sentiment and poetry. Davies was an artist of wide culture and fine taste, a sort of contemporary John La Farge. He did much to create a broader and finer appreciation of art, and many splendid collections, such as that of Lillie P. Bliss, owe a good deal to his taste and judgment. More than any other artist he was responsible for the Armory Show of 1913, an exhibition of revolutionary importance for American art. Davies responded to the major influences in the art of his time. He was an experimenter who tried his hand at all the current "isms" and all sorts of mediums, oil painting, watercolor, pastel, sculpture, tapestry and a variety of print mediums. His earlier paintings

are probably his best (*Every Saturday*). For all his experimenting he remained to the end a peculiarly American romanticist, steeped in the tradition of "seeing beautifully."

Close to Henri in their beginnings are John Sloan and George Luks, and George Bellows, a younger man who joined the Henri group later than the other two. Sloan is a fine draughtsman and is the most distinguished of contemporary American etchers, master of a multilinear technique unmistakably his own. He studied at the Pennsylvania Academy of the Fine Arts and got the influence of Eakins through Thomas P. Anschutz. He is a keen observer of contemporary American life, in technique and point of view somewhat akin to the English satirists, Hogarth, Keene and Leech. He has a realistic fidelity to the facts of American city life, which he sees with honesty tinged with a bitter irony. Sloan has progressed from his earlier im-

HENRI   The Art Institute of Chicago
YOUNG WOMAN IN BLACK

DAVIES
EVERY SATURDAY

The Brooklyn Museum

pressionism, in which are recollections of Whistler, to a fuller, more solid structure and a higher-keyed palette. In later years he has done a good deal of technical experimenting, but many of his best works (*McSorley's Bar, The Wake of the Ferry,* [Phillips Memorial Gallery, Washington, D. C.]) are in his earlier manner. His teaching, with its strong emphasis upon localism, native tradition, and sound craftsmanship, has profoundly influenced the younger generation of American artists.

George Luks studied at the Pennsylvania Academy of the Fine Arts and in Paris and Düsseldorf. He was a political caricaturist, and a newspaper illustrator during the war with Spain. He was a manipulator of paint, a devotee of the slashing stroke, and while his work has force and a richer tonality than that of many members of his group, it is uneven and often too summary, as if he lacked the patience to continue. At his best he had verve and gusto, the flash of the moment seen for its own sake, without much profundity. He painted good portraits, and his pictures of children, such as *The Spielers,* are excellent in their spontaneous and sympathetic caricature.

George Bellows, a pupil of Henri, had a broad, swift technique and a great deal of vigor and masculinity. Bellows died young, but he made a tremendous impression and was by far the most popular artist of his group. He was a man's man, the he-man of American art in a time of too many soft painters. Frankly absorbed in contemporary subject matter, he gave powerful emphasis to the doctrine of "painting American" which had already been stressed by Sloan and Henri and which has become a text for a large group of painters today. Bellows

seldom tried to be ingratiating in choice of subject, in method or in color. His transcripts from the American scene are harsh and powerful in execution as well as in vision. He was an excellent technician in the lithographic medium and a distinguished contributor to American illustration. Among his best and most characteristic works are his paintings and lithographs of sporting life. (See color plate No. I.)

Other artists whose work relates them to the Henri group are Glenn O. Coleman, Rockwell Kent, Jerome Myers and George Overbury Hart. Coleman's work constitutes one of the most complete pictorial records of changing New York (*Angelo's Place*). Most commentators on the American scene since Henri have been rather grim about it. Coleman contributes a welcome note of whimsicality, especially in his lithographs which are as rich, as moving, and as quaint as Currier & Ives prints at their best. Rockwell Kent expresses the spirit of American life in a harsh, romantic symbolism, and is important as print maker and illustrator. Jerome Myers is the poet of city streets, a mellow, kindly commentator on the teeming life of New York's East Side. He has a very personal sense of color. George Overbury Hart, a self-taught artist whose best work is in watercolors and prints, was a kind of contemporary Winslow Homer. He had something of Homer's broad realism and his sturdy American individualism. One feels that Hart, like Henri, loved people, and while he had a keen eye for the queerness and drabness of life it never moved him to bitterness or satire. He had a stronger feeling for the impact and humor of the grotesque than any other artist of our time (*Merry-Go-Round*). As a print maker he had few equals.

The greatest importance of the Henri group was in opening the eyes of American artists to the life around them, to contemporary and local subject matter.

SLOAN
McSorley's Bar

The Detroit Institute o

COLEMAN
ANGELO'S PLACE

Private Collection, New York

MYERS
CHRISTMAS DINNER

Collection Arthur F. Egner

LUKS
THE SPIELERS

Addison Gallery of American Art, Andover, Mass.

They brought the gusty vitality of common living into the staid atmosphere of the academies. They did much toward improving and liberalizing art teaching in this country, and were leaders in all movements for an open forum in American art. In 1910 they organized a large exhibition which was independent both of official academies and dealers, they sponsored the Armory Show of 1913, and the Society of Independent Artists which was founded in 1917. These independent movements had become very necessary in the first decade of the twentieth century. The Society of American Artists had joined forces with the Academy in 1906. There was now no organized opposition and the academicians had things their own way. The younger and more advanced painters were faced with the same alternative as the men of the 1870's. They had to form exhibition groups of their own or go without recognition.

· 33 ·

ART
MERRY-GO-ROUND

Private Collection, New York

V. THE IMPACT OF MODERN ART

THE MOST vital tendencies in American art today were set by the Henri group and by the modernists who came into prominence between 1910 and 1920. "The Eight" were important in forming the point of view of contemporary painters who draw their inspiration directly from the American scene. The modernists sounded the retreat from the "back to nature" movement and raised the opposing slogan of "back to the museum." The naturalistic movement had been pushed by the Impressionists as far as it seemed profitable and by the end of the nineteenth century a reaction had set in.

This reaction was based largely on the endeavor of Paul Cézanne to achieve through a broader application of Impressionism an order as solid and satisfying as that of the Renaissance masters. Cézanne was concerned with architectonic composition, and wanted to fuse the Impressionists' brilliant observation of light, color and surface with a feeling for the underlying structure and solidity of form. He abandoned the "little touches" of Impressionism, broadened his areas of color, and devised a method of color modeling which emphasizes the separation of planes, suggests their movement forward and back, and thus leads the eye into deep space. He completed the research in color chiaroscuro as distinguished from the traditional chiaroscuro of light and shade, a research which had been carried on by Impressionist painters from the time of Manet. Cézanne has been one of the most powerful influences in European and American art for the past thirty years. His emphasis upon structure and solidity turned contemporary art toward the great European tradition of design, to a renewed concern with an ordered relation of forms in space, rather than with making exact records of the momentary look of objects, or of fleeting effects of light.

Cézanne's return to the "art of the museums," to the ideas of the baroque and Renaissance masters, was carried further back and further afield by later Post-Impressionists, by the *Fauves,* or "wild animals" group, and by the Cubists. These painters explored the European tradition in the light of Oriental and primitive art. In medieval, Byzantine, Greek, Egyptian, Persian, Hindu, Chinese, Japanese, African, Polynesian, and ancient American art they discovered greater freedom in the treatment of broad areas of flat color, the use of black outlines, tilted and diagonal perspective, rhythmic design, and a variety of non-naturalistic, abstract and decorative modes of expression. In their reaction against naturalism the modernists came to believe, as Maurice Denis has said, "that every work of art is a caricature, a passionate interpretation of a sensation." They insisted that a painting is essentially a "plane surface covered with colors set down in a certain order" and that subject or "human interest" is a comparatively unimportant matter. All this by way of emphasizing the fact that the aim of painting is the creation of an emotionally appreciable order, and that this order must be achieved within the limitations of the painter's medium. Some, like the Cubists, were lured by geometry and by the distortions and simplifications of form in the art of primitive and savage peoples. Others, like certain members of the *Fauves,* the Expressionists, and the Super-realists (who came later), were not allured by the cold splendors of geometry. They stressed the imaginative and personal, sought "to create a new vision" and to cultivate a sensibility attuned to the unexpected, the mysterious, the fantastic, and the macabre.

The modern movement followed many trails. A few of these trails led nowhere in particular, but the main road was a good one. It led back to the sources of tradition. Previous movements of the nineteenth century had emphasized nature. The modernists stressed design, structure, organization, the abstract qualities of art. The emphasis upon abstraction carried some of them very far—to the point where they banished subject completely. This phase of the modernist endeavor appears to have passed into the decorative arts and architecture, at least so far as America is concerned. Other modernists at-

WEBER
NEW YORK AT NIGHT

Collection the Artist

STELLA
PORT OF NEW YORK

Collection the Artist

it was something to laugh at, but to a large group of the younger artists it was a blare of trumpets against the Jericho of academism. Galleries devoted to modern art came into being. Publications to champion the new tendencies were founded. Pulses were quickened. The life of art seemed worth while. But the World War dampened the ardor of the first impulse, and it was not until 1920 that modernism was at full tide in America.

The pioneers of the modern movement in this country were Max Weber, Alfred H. Maurer, Samuel Halpert, John Marin, Bernard Karfiol, William and Marguerite Zorach, Thomas Benton, McDonald Wright, Morgan Russell, Abraham Walkowitz and Walt Kuhn. Most of these painters had studied in Paris before 1912. Access to modernist ideas was easy for American artists in Paris. Among the first propagandists for modern art, aside from the painters, were the American writer, Gertrude Stein, and her brother, Leo Stein. Their house in Paris was a center for the discussion of the new ideas.

The earliest of the group were Max Weber, John Marin, Alfred H. Maurer, Bernard Karfiol, Samuel Halpert and Abraham Walkowitz. These men all came into contact with the diverse currents of modernist ideas in the first decade of the century. Weber, who had been a pupil of Arthur Dow in New York and Matisse in Paris, and an intimate of the customs officer, Rousseau, is one of the keenest intelligences in modern art, a man who has run the gamut of contemporary expression. No other American artist has made a more profound study of his medium than has Weber, or searched more thoroughly the possibilities of abstract and emotional expression. He is a born colorist, and expresses in his art a deeply racial and religious strain. In his later work he achieves a fine solution of the problems of the relation of form and concept, realism and abstraction.

Marin, whose art developed in this country, has been called the greatest watercolorist of the American tradition. No other painter of our time approaches him in masterly handling of the medium. He has an extraordinary personal shorthand in which he summarizes a broad, penetrating and dramatic vision of nature in a few lines and washes. The arbitrary freedom of his style gives his work a vivid aliveness, an almost explosive force. For all his summariness Marin has both clarity and order, and a decorative sense which shows in his arrangements and in his fine use of color. (*Stonington, Maine*, see color plate No. VII.) Maurer (1868-

tempted to imitate primitive and naïve folk expression. This work, save for that of a few rare souls whose naïvete needed no fillip from fashion, has proved of doubtful value. But there can be no question that modernism has exerted a powerful and vitalizing influence upon contemporary art, both in Europe and America. It has given art in this country a wider range of knowledge and a firmer basis in tradition.

Modernism, or rather Post-Impressionism, Cubism, Futurism and Expressionism, burst upon the American public in the epoch-making New York Armory Show of 1913. This exhibition, one of the landmarks of American art,

was organized by an association of painters and sculptors under the presidency of Arthur B. Davies. A number of American and French modernists were already known to a limited public. Two photographers, Alfred Stieglitz and Edward Steichen, were the first to bring the work of European modernists to this country. Beginning as early as 1908 Stieglitz had displayed modern works in his gallery at 291 Fifth Avenue, the most important center for the dissemination of modernist ideas in America. The Armory Show brought these ideas before a wider public. Most critics and artists greeted the show with ridicule and abuse. To the great American public

WEBER
BEAUTIFICATION

Collection the Artist

sionists than he is to the Post-Impressionist group. He is one of the best of contemporary figure painters, a fine draughtsman and a colorist who uses a very carefully thought-out method of color gradation with which he gets fullness of form and tenderness of modeling. He is essentially a poet, robust yet sensitive. His art, like Twachtman's, achieves strength without the slightest over-emphasis or bombast. Halpert (1884-1930), like Weber, was an artist of sound training, who developed an honest and unarbitrary style after he had shaken off the influence of the National Academy of Design and of his Parisian teacher, Bonnat. His work is spontaneous, unlabored and simple, and shows a good color sense and authoritative arrangement. Walkowitz, one of the earliest modernists to show in this country, is a watercolorist whose best work is in flower paintings and in poetic interpretations of proletarian types. Lately he has been much concerned with linear abstractions of city scenes.

After the Armory Show the American art world became a battleground for modernist and academic ideas. Many group shows of modern works were organized and each group issued its defiant manifesto. About 1914 McDonald Wright and Morgan Russell launched their short-lived "Synchromist" movement. Seen in the perspective of the years Synchromisn seems mildly decora-

1932), son of one of the most famous makers of Currier & Ives prints, had something of Marin's arbitrary freedom. He started out as a Whistlerian, but after he had won a few prizes in this manner he remade his art in the fires of *Fauvism* into a mode of expression which records something of the intensity and strain of modern life.

Karfiol is closer to the later Impres-

KARFIOL
THREE SEATED FIGURES

Collection Dr. B. D. Saklatwalla, Pittsburgh

tive, but in 1914 it created considerable stir. Since that time very little has been heard of McDonald Wright or Morgan Russell. One of the most active propagandists for modern art was Walt Kuhn who was closely associated with Arthur B. Davies in organizing the Armory Show. Kuhn is a figure and landscape painter who shows a good deal of power, especially in his later work. He is a keen observer of contemporary city types, and achieves intensity of expression through simplification and emphasis. (*The Blue Clown,* see color plate No. III.) William Zorach will be discussed in the article on sculpture but his contribution in watercolor, a medium which he handles with distinction, cannot be disregarded. Marguerite Zorach has made a contribution both as painter and as the creator of a style in tapestry embroidery. Thomas Benton will be considered with the mural painters.

The range and variety of modern art in this country is illustrated in the work of such men as Charles Demuth, Preston Dickinson, Maurice Sterne, Henry Lee McFee, Marsden Hartley, Arthur Dove, Andrew Dasburg and Joseph Stella. Demuth, like Marin, is a stylist. An artist of sure taste, inventive and precise in his design, and pleasing in color, he yields only to Marin in his masterly handling of the watercolor medium. In some of his work, especially the architectural scenes, he uses a very delicate kind of Cubism. He has a feeling for the human episode, when he chooses to be concerned with it, that makes his illustrations the best things of their kind produced in this country. Preston Dickinson (1891-1930), whose early death was a severe loss to American art, was a clever designer with an almost Oriental feeling for spatial arrangement and refined color. Next to Mary Cassatt he was the greatest American virtuoso in the pastel medium. (*Still Life,* see color plate No. VI.) The modernism of Maurice Sterne is tempered by a viewpoint essentially classic. He is one of the finest draughtsmen in contemporary American art. In landscapes and figure paintings, and in sculpture, he shows a thorough understanding of the relation of form and space. (*Girl in Blue Chair,* color plate No. V.) Somewhat akin to Sterne in his concern with ordered formal relationships is Henry Lee McFee. He is a sound, intellectual artist who paints in low-toned harmonies and gets unusually good quality of surface and texture. Marsden Hartley is an artist of fine taste who has experimented in various modes and is one of the few Americans who have produced interesting abstract paintings. Arthur Dove is a romanticist of the abstract and has a very pleasing color

HALPERT
CHECKERED CLOTH

The Detroit Institute of Arts

sense. Another experimenter in abstraction is Andrew Dasburg, the outstanding artist of the Santa Fe group. However, in recent years, with many of the earlier modernists, Dasburg has turned from abstraction to a more realistic approach to landscape. Joseph Stella, who has lived abroad for a number of years, has a dynamic and decorative style which emphasizes linear movement. In putting together several views of a subject in the same picture Stella brought a note of Italian Futurism into American art. (See page 35.)

There is a group of painters which interprets the contemporary American scene in a highly selective realism, amounting almost to a formal purism. Leading representatives of this group are such artists as Charles Sheeler, Georgia O'Keeffe, Peter Blume, and Niles Spencer. Charles Sheeler is one of the most lucid draughtsmen among American artists today. The dominant characteristics of his style are sound realism, clarity, and austerely selective vision. His work has something of the strong, simple construction, the severe beauty and fitness of engineering design. Georgia O'Keeffe expresses her reaction to American life in a symbolism that is both rich and clear. While her best known work is in flower painting, her landscapes and her pictures of early American architecture, with their feeling for great, clear spaces and beautiful proportion, have vitality of conception and an unmistakable personal quality. Peter Blume is a remarkably fine craftsman who always gets a highly finished surface and a telling pattern of light and dark. He has something of the Super-

DEMUTH
ILLUSTRATION FOR *The Turn of the Screw*

Collection Frank Osborn, New York

SHEELER
AMERICAN LANDSCAPE

Private Collection, New York

McFEE
CORNER OF THE STUDIO

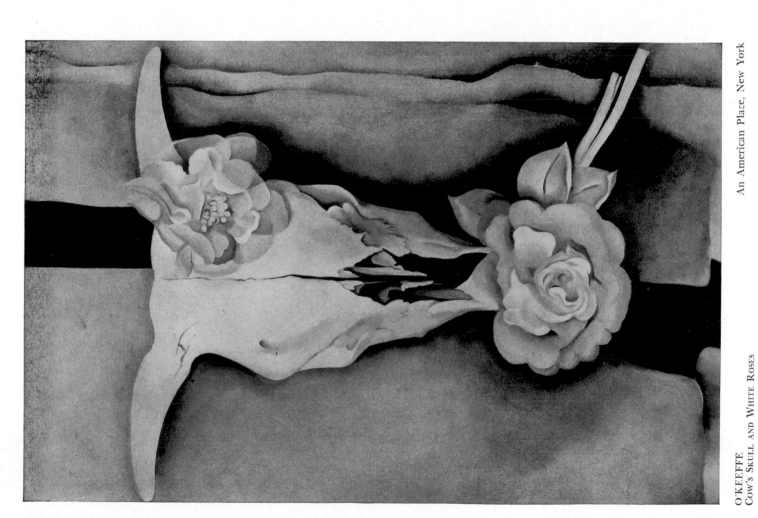

O'KEEFFE
COW'S SKULL AND WHITE ROSES

BLUME
SOUTH OF SCRANTON

Collection the Artist

He has a thoroughly clear conception of what he wants to do, and he depicts a severely selected version of the American scene with a stark emotional integrity which sometimes admits a hint of satire in handling the architectural remains of the near past. He has done good work in landscape and figure painting and is one of the best print makers today. (*Lighthouse at Two Lights,* color plate No. II) Charles Burchfield, a watercolorist, is more romantic and emotional than Hopper. He is the historian of what is most typically, and one might say tragically, American in the characterful ugliness of small towns. His early work was romantic and to an extent, literary. His later work is more decorative and realisitic. (*Tile Roof,* see color plate No. VIII) Reginald Marsh is essentially of today, registering the look and movement of city crowds. He has a keen eye for significant detail and with more clarity of conception and a more thoroughly thought-out structure may develop into a painter of real power. John Steuart Curry, the genre painter of the Middle West, is as American as a Kansas wheat field. He is a self-taught artist still in the making who has a great deal of dramatic force. Peggy Bacon's pastel portraits of contemporary celebrities are excellent in their searching and acid caricature. She is one of the best contemporary etchers. Guy Pène DuBois presents a hard-boiled version of modern city types in rather pleasing color. Boardman Robinson has done excellent work in social caricature, and recently has turned to mural painting. With this group we may include such artists as Harry Gottlieb, George Picken, Randall Davey, Bertram Hartman, David Morri-

realists' feeling for the unexpected, and can make a strongly knit design out of seemingly unrelated architectural units and fantastic fragments of episode. Niles Spencer's work has clarity of conception, sound construction, good textural quality, and a rich harmony of low tones. Stefan Hirsch has a good sense of decorative formal harmony. Lately, he has become interested in mural painting. Stuart Davis, one of the most intelligent and inventive of American experimenters in abstraction, appears to be turning to an art of richer human documentation. The work of George Ault, Arnold Wiltz, Henry Billings, Charles Goeller, Francis Criss and Elsie Driggs, is characterized by clarity of design and excellent feeling for architectonic arrangement.

More frankly realistic is the work of such artists as Eugene Speicher, Edward Hopper, John Steuart Curry, Charles Burchfield, Guy Pène DuBois, Boardman Robinson, Peggy Bacon, and other painters who are clearly related to the earlier Henri group. Among these artists are several excellent portrait painters. There has been no portrait school in this country since the early Republican period, though there have been many individual portraitists of solid accomplishment. The contemporary standard bearer is Eugene

Speicher who may be considered the leading portrait painter, and one of the soundest figure painters, in this country today. His work has realistic honesty, structural gravity and sober color. (*Babette,* see color plate No. IV) Edward Hopper has written that his aim is to make the most exact possible transcription of his impressions of nature.

SPENCER
ORDNANCE ISLAND, BERMUDA

Collection Mr. and Mrs. Samuel A. Lewisohn, New York

son, H. E. Schnakenberg and Richard Lahey.

A lyrical and romantic note appears in the work of such painters as Yasuo Kuniyoshi, Alexander Brook, Ernest Fiene, Franklin C. Watkins, Joseph Pollet, Morris Kantor, Anne Goldthwaite, Arnold Blanch, Henry Varnum Poor, Dorothy Varian, Henry Mattson and others. Kuniyoshi's style has in it elements of modernism and Oriental art, and something of the spirit of the American folk painters. Kuniyoshi solves, for himself at least, the problem of fusing the traditions of East and West, a problem which baffled such artists as Whistler and La Farge. Brook is an able technician and one of the few contemporaries who handles paint as if he really enjoyed it. He is a strong designer, and gets rich color in subdued tones, and unusually interesting textural quality. (*Isis.* See color plate No. IX) Fiene, also, is a very able technician, whose thoroughly sound realism is tempered by an essentially romantic point of view. Watkins, the most extreme romanticist among these painters, reflects in his art something of the chaos and unrest of modern life. The freshness and vigor of Joseph Pollet's early style have been somewhat diminished in recent years. He appears to be in a period of indecision, aspiring possibly to create a new version of the great style of the late Renaissance. Anne Goldthwaite has an effortless and charming impressionism, particularly effective in depicting scenes from Southern life which she records with keen perception. Kantor has come through diverse modern influences to a style characterized by inventiveness, good color and quality of surface. Var-

HIRSCH
NEW YORK

Phillips Memorial Gallery, Washington, D. C.

num Poor is a gifted technician whose work has both simplicity and charm. Dorothy Varian's work has a rich sensitive quality and fresh and joyous color. Henry Mattson, one of the leading members of the Woodstock group, has a dreamy, poetic note which shows at its best in landscape.

An accent upon objectivity, upon exactly defined forms clearly and simply related, is present in the work of many of the artists we have been discussing. It is evident in the work of Kathrine Schmidt whose subject matter is the Victorian-baroque. The objectivist point of view is evident also in the work of such men as Harry W. Watrous and Luigi Lucioni. Watrous is a masterly technician, concerned mostly with still life. The contemporary quality of his work is obscured, somewhat, by his choice of subject matter.

The well-advertised American standardization has never been very thoroughly enforced in the arts. There have always been originals difficult to fit into any group. Today we have such originals as Louis Eilshemius, Florine Stettheimer, Arnold Friedman, Emile Branchard, Julia Kelly and John Kane. Eilshemius, painter, poet, playwright, composer, is an artist almost as prolific as Rubens. Naïve in vision and romantic in style, Eilshemius has a note of unexpectedness and fantasy which is very delightful. Altogether he is one of the most extraordinary "singulars" in contemporary American art. Friedman is a poetic painter who composes with large flat areas of color somewhat after the Chinese mode of line and local tone. Florine Stettheimer, who gets very subtle harmonies with broad areas of highkeyed color, has a genuine decorative talent. Her stage decorations for the

opera, *Four Saints in Three Acts,* constitute the most original contribution to American theater design in recent years. Branchard is a painter of the naïve school. His work is uneven, but he sometimes gets distinguished pattern and a pleasing balance of flat tones. The work of Julia Kelly, another naïve painter, has the spontaneity and freshness of a child's view of nature. John Kane (1859-1934) was definitely in the tradition of American folk art. His sincerity and his interest in his subject matter give his paintings a poetic if rather quaint charm, in spite of technical deficiencies. One might include with the folk painters the Indian artists of the Southwest, Fred Kabotie, Awa Tsireh, Ogwa Pi and others, who in the past few years have been producing pictures, mainly watercolors, which are valuable documents on the ceremonial life of the Southwestern tribes, and interesting as showing the Indian's natural feeling for the abstract and the decorative.

The work of most of the artists mentioned in this article, even that of the Indians, has been affected by the modern movement. Modern art, particularly of the French school, has been the dominant influence upon the younger generation of American painters. In late years there have been signs of rebellion against the French influence, and a demand that American art free itself of foreign entanglements. The question of influences has always been a difficult one in any discussion of the American situation. American art was transplanted from Europe and throughout its history has reacted to European influences. Nevertheless, from the time of Inness to our own, American artists have been scolded for accepting hints from the contemporary practice of Europe. The curious part of this business is that each generation of critics and collectors has approved the European influence as long as it was that of artists who had been dead long enough. The men who criticized Inness thought the Düsseldorf influence quite all right, but could say nothing too severe about Corot. The American followers of the Barbizon painters could see little in Impressionism, though both Inness and Martin in their late manner were affected by it. Impressionists and academicians both turned in fury on the advance guard of modernism. But modern art made its way in spite of opposition. Today, most major museums in this country have opened their doors to it. The Museum of Modern Art in New York, is devoted to the more advanced tendencies in American and European art, and the Whitney Museum of American Art in New York has been very hospitable to modern artists.

VI. THE CONTEMPORARY AMERICAN WORLD

EACH generation in art is characterized by its emphasis upon certain methods and ideas. It is true that diverse tendencies are present in any epoch. There is always an interweaving of strands, but definite directions may usually be discerned. In spite of divergent trends and counter movements the leading tendencies have been fairly clear in the various periods of American art which have been discussed in this radio series. In Colonial times the aristocratic portrait in the style of the English school was the thing, yielding somewhat in the early Republican period to historical painting in the manner of Benjamin West and to the studio mythologies of French classicism. In the decades immediately before the Civil War there was the dialect accent of the provincial genre and portrait painters, and the

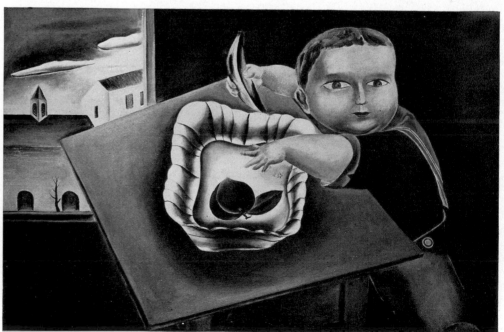

KUNIYOSHI
BOY STEALING FRUIT

The Columbus Gallery of Fine Arts

more self-conscious localism of the Hudson River men and the painters of spectacular landscape.

Since the Civil War we have seen the strain of American localism running through the work of Winslow Homer, Thomas Eakins, John Sloan, George Bellows, Edward Hopper and others. With this there has been a succession of waves of European influence, mainly French, from the romantic naturalism of the Barbizon painters, through the more scientific naturalism of the Impressionists, to what might be called the abstract realism of the modernists with their emphasis upon an emotionally appreciable order imposed on nature by man.

The present generation of American painters has passed through an era of technical research which appears to be ended. For twenty years our artists have been predominantly concerned with the means of expression. They have experimented with every conceivable device for handling form and color. On the whole it has been a magnificent research. Now arises the not unimportant question: what is the artist to do with it all? What has he to say with it? It is a knotty question. In these matters hindsight is better than foresight. The roads of yesterday are comparatively clear. The way of tomorrow is shadowed by uncertainties.

There is no current from Europe today comparable in power to Impressionism or Post-Impressionism. It would seem that the School of Paris has yielded its world hegemony. In any event, there is a demand in this country for a distinctive note of Americanism. American art

FIENE
HUDSON NAVIGATION BOAT

Whitney Museum of American Art, New York

is declaring a moratorium on its debts to Europe, and turning to cultivate its own garden. The standard of nationalism has been raised and following that the standard of regionalism. All this is a healthy reaction against eclectic tendencies, but it can be carried too far. Ernest Fenollosa, one of the most brilliant of American art critics, has pointed out that foreign influence is invariably at the heart of the native development. This was just as true of classical Greece and Rome, or Renaissance Italy and Spain, as it is of modern America.

Today we are in a position somewhat similar to that of the period just after the Civil War. But today there is not the same yeasty optimism or economic romanticism. There are no more economic worlds to conquer, no West to win. The circle of manifest destiny has been completed. We are living in a time of conscious and critical revaluation, of profound readjustments. In the depression art seems more a luxury than ever, the artist more divorced from life. And there are no avenues of escape. There is no Europe, no Tahiti, no Bohemia, no ivory tower safe from the encroachments of the world. The Olympus of the observer, detached from the actualities of daily living, has been blasted out of existence. Art for art's sake is a tattered banner which has blown down the wind. There is no health in introspection.

WATKINS
SUICIDE IN COSTUME

Collection Albert C. Lehman, Pittsburgh

· 43 ·

EILSHEMIUS
SUNSET, SAMOA

Valentine Gallery, New York

The cultivation of sensibility has become a blind alley.

All these things have been considered by contemporary American painters. The reactions vary. Some painters, like Stuart Davis, Karl Knaths, Arshile Gorky and John D. Graham, are still concerned with the problems of abstract painting, and there has recently been a renascence of interest in abstraction among a group of the younger men. Some, like certain members of the Woodstock group, have been turning to the romanticism of the 1830's which was such a vital force in nineteenth century art. Others, like the "Americana school," appear to have taken to heart the saying of Fromentin about the

GAG
THE FORGE (Lithograph)

Dutch that to be artists they need only paint the portrait of their own country. Still others, finding that abstraction has reached the point of diminishing returns, that nineteenth century romanticism is worked out, and dissatisfied with merely reflecting the strain and chaos of the contemporary world, are groping for some unifying philosophy which shall give their art coherence and meaning.

The one clear note in contemporary American painting is a new emphasis upon social and collective expression. Subject and "human interest" have definitely been reinstated in art. This appears not only in easel painting but also in murals and in American prints which give a fresh and vital interpretation of

FIENE
MADISON SQUARE PARK (Etching)

life as it is lived in this country. There are fewer studio subjects, fewer still life paintings. There are more portraits, figures in action and crowd scenes. A few years ago modern American artists, with one or two exceptions, seemed incapable of painting portraits. Today there are many good portrait painters among the younger men, especially among the pupils of John Sloan and Kenneth Hayes Miller. (Miller, a pupil of Chase and a thorough student of painting, has exerted a strong influence upon the younger generation of artists. He is an accomplished figure painter interested in contemporary subjects.)

Once more man is the most interesting subject of the artist. The impact of the present moment in all its tragedy and confusion, its bewildering surfaces and its disturbing emotional quality has forced upon the artist a concern with the problems of human society. There is a demand that the artist have something to say relevant to the life of today and that he say it with clarity and force. The most intelligent artists realize that it is not enough merely to illustrate ideas which are currently popular and to treat them in such a way as to appeal to contemporary prejudice or easily uncovered emotion. That would be to follow the path of popular illustration, to reflect the spirit of the age at its lowest intensity. The significance of the work of art must exist not only in its reaction to life but also in its form. For if it is true that contemporary life is the artist's environment, it is also true that the great tradition of art is his inheritance. He neglects either at his peril.

Samuel Isham, writing thirty years ago, could say: "Two or three centuries from now those curious to learn what manner of people lived at the beginning of the twentieth century can cull from the art production of France, or Germany, or of England an infinity of pictures, many of high artistic merit, that will give them the very age and body of the time. From America they will get hardly anything of the sort, at least in oil painting." The statement is only partly true. Winslow Homer had depicted the life of his period. Frederick Remington, the chronicler of the Wild West, had set down with direct if crude force the very age and body of the cowboy era. Thomas Hovenden (the favorite artist of William Jennings Bryan), J. G. Brown and E. L. Henry, in their story-telling pictures of the lives of humble folk and of the sorrows and humors of street urchins, had uncovered the vein of homely sentiment which lies so near the surface of American character. The work of illustrators like F. O. C. Darley, A. B. Frost and Charles Dana Gibson is a key to the spirit of their times. John Sloan, George Bellows, Glenn Coleman, Boardman Robinson and others, have given us a richly documented history of the life of city streets in the last thirty years, not only in their paintings but also in their prints and in the caricatures which they contributed to various publications, notably the old *Masses*.

SOCIAL AND POLITICAL CARICATURE

America, with its free and easy politics, its dramatic contrasts of poverty and wealth, should be a rich field for the social and political caricaturist, but very little has been produced in this country comparable to the best European caricature. Thomas Nast (1840-1902) did splendid work in the 1870's, and had a

ARMS   Kennedy & Co.
GOTHIC GLORY (Etching)

tremendous effect on public opinion, especially in his attacks on the Tweed Ring in New York. He had successors who excelled him in draughtsmanship, but not in power. There are a number of able caricaturists today, Art Young, the dean of the old *Masses* group, Rollin Kirby of the New York *World-Telegram*, Oscar Cesare of the *New York Times*, Edmond Duffy of the Baltimore *Sun*, Peter Arno, Otto Soglow and James Thurber of the *New Yorker*, William Gropper and Hugo Gellert of the *New Masses*. The most powerful social caricature today is that of William Gropper, who is also a good painter. No contemporary excels Al Frueh in draughtsmanship and quaint humor, and none excels Robert Minor in dramatic force, but these men have produced little in recent

years. In the comic strips excellent work has been done by Rudy Dirks, Cliff Sterrett, George Herriman and Percy Crosby.

The quality of caricature and of illustration in this country has been lowered by the headlong speed and quantity production methods of printing and the need, real or fancied, for publications to fit their policy to the lowest common denominator of intelligence. The best social comment today is that of the print makers, artists who are not limited by the technical standards and the conventional point of view of newspapers and magazines.

THE PRINT MAKERS

Prints have been an important phase of American expression in the arts since the 1830's. From that time up to the 1890's the prints of Currier & Ives and other makers were popular. However, interest in print making as an art suffered a decline toward the close of the century. Lithography went out of fashion almost entirely because of the cheap commercialism which followed the success of Currier & Ives. The only print medium which had any reputation was etching. Outstanding among the American etchers of the nineteenth century are Whistler, Duveneck, Twachtman and Mary Cassatt. William Morris Hunt was an excellent lithographer, though the reputation of Whistler far exceeded Hunt's modest fame. Whistler had a feeling for delicate variations of tone which is the essence of lithography, but most of his lithographs are really drawings, since they were made on paper

PENNELL   Keppel & Co.
APPROACHES TO GATUN LOCK (Lithograph)

and later transferred to the stone. Joseph Pennell (1860-1926) was a skillful technician both in etching and lithography, and as a teacher at the Art Students League he had an influence for sound craftsmanship upon the younger print makers of today.

In the past two decades there has been a growth of public interest in prints and a remarkable development in all branches of the art, particularly in lithography. Today every type of medium has able practitioners—drypoint, etching,

COLEMAN   The Downtown Gallery, New York
HURDY-GURDY (Lithograph)

LOCKE
THE GALLERY (Lithograph)

BELLOWS
DANCE IN A MADHOUSE (Lithograph)
Whitney Museum of American Art, New York

MILLER
LEAVING THE SHOP (Etching)

HART
THE JURY (Lithograph)
The Downtown Gallery, New York

BACON   The Downtown Gallery, New York
THE PATRONESS (Etching)

CURRY
THE TORNADO (Lithograph)

KENT
MEDITATION (Lithograph)

WALKOWITZ
BROOKLYN (Lithograph)

soft ground, aquatint, lithography, lithotint, wood engraving, and other print mediums in black and white and in color. Technically, the English etchers are still superior to the Americans, and the Germans outrank them in wood engraving. In lithography, aquatint, and soft ground etching the Americans lead.

Most of the leading artists in this country have done important work in one or more print mediums, and have brought to this art something of the larger spirit of painting, an abler and freer draughtsmanship, an emphasis upon design, originality of conception and inventiveness. Painters like George Bellows, Kenneth Hayes Miller, George O. Hart, Max Weber, Arthur B. Davies, Edward Hopper, John Marin, Albert Sterner, Rockwell Kent, Frank W. Benson, Eugene Higgins, Childe Hassam, Peggy Bacon, Reginald Marsh, Alexander Brook, Ernest Fiene and Louis Lozowick have made important contributions in etching and lithography. John Taylor Arms, Ernest D. Roth, Harry Wickey, Martin Lewis and William Auerbach-Levy are remarkably fine technicians in etching. Emil Ganso is an able technician in all the print mediums, and Charles Locke is one of the best lithographers. An entire period of American life is recorded in the etchings and lithographs of John Sloan and Glenn Coleman.

Contemporary American prints are rich in social content. Every aspect of the American scene is reflected, the cities with their medley of architectural styles, skyscrapers, gasoline tanks, subways, crowds in the street, the great harbors, interiors of homes of every social class, prairie farms, city apartments, mountaineer cabins, factories, mines, grain elevators, wheat fields, sports, politics and a hundred other subjects. Among the artists not otherwise mentioned who have done excellent work in print making are: George Constant, Howard Cook, Lewis C. Daniel, Adolph Dehn, Isami Doi, Mabel Dwight, Kerr Eby, Eugene Fitsch, Karl Free, Don Freeman, Wanda Gag, H. Glintenkamp, Thomas Handforth, Rosella Hartman, A. Z. Kruse, Max Kuehne, J. J. Lankes, Margaret Lowengrund, Austin Mecklem, William Meyerowitz, William C. McNulty, John J. A. Murphy, Fred Nagler, Ralph Pearson, Philip Reisman, Robert Riggs, Doris Rosenthal, Andrée Ruellan, Rudolph Ruzicka, Arnold Ronnebeck, Alexander Stavenitz, Harry Sternberg, Prentiss Taylor and Stow Wengenroth.

MURAL PAINTING

The contemporary emphasis upon human significance in art gets its strongest expression in mural painting. There have been signs during the past decade that the easel picture might be ousted from its dominant position by the mural. The fame of the Mexican painters has had something to do with this. More important is the demand for social and collective expression which seems better suited to the mural than to the easel picture, the renewed interest in the decorative function of art which is one of the products of modernism, and the virtual disappearance of the private patron in a time of economic stress. The mural has become a live issue, and this renascence of interest in wall painting has been focused by the work of Rivera, Orozco, Charlot and Siqueiros in this country, by exhibitions at The Museum of Modern Art in New York, by various public art projects which have engaged artists to decorate public buildings, and by the work of such American painters as Thomas Benton and Boardman Robinson.

Mural painting in one form or another has been practised in America since the early eighteenth century. Many houses in New England and Virginia had painted interiors. Gustavus Hesselius' *Last Supper* for St. Barnabus' Church, Queen Anne Parish, Maryland, was painted in 1721. John Trumbull and John Vanderlyn painted enlarged easel pictures for the Capitol at Washington, beginning in 1824. Constantino Brumidi, an Italian refugee, and a number of his compatriots worked in the dome of the Capitol in the 1850's. Emanuel Leutze painted his *Star of Empire* for the Capitol in 1859. In spite of all this work American mural decoration offered little of interest until Henry Hobson Richardson engaged John La Farge to decorate the interior of Trinity Church,

BENTON
ARTS OF THE WEST

From series of murals, Whitney Museum of American Art, New York

ROBINSON
SERMON ON THE MOUNT (Fresco)

Collection Eugene Schoen, Inc., New York

many other artists, and by virtue of his efforts in this field he assumes importance. His murals for the New School for Social Research and the Whitney Museum of American Art in New York, and for the Indiana State Building at the Century of Progress exposition in Chicago, are typical of his style. The decorations of Boardman Robinson for the Kaufmann Department Store in Pittsburgh and for Rockefeller Center in New York lack the force of Benton's work, but they are genuine contributions to American mural art. Stuart Davis and Yasuo Kuniyoshi have shown distinct talent in their decorations at Rockefeller Center, but the scope of their work was severely limited. Louis Bouché, Jane Berlandina, George Biddle, Henry Billings, Clarence Carter, Stefan Hirsch, Ben Shahn and Grant Wood have shown definite promise, and such painters as Charles Sheeler, Max Weber, Georgia O'Keeffe, Bernard Karfiol, Ernest Fiene, Reginald Marsh, Franklin C. Watkins and many others might very well produce excellent murals if given the opportunity.

What American mural painters need most of all is walls. This need has been met to some extent by various public art projects, federal and state, but since these were connected with a relief program not many of the leading artists were engaged. Still, it appears that considerable good work has been done on these projects, though it is too early adequately to measure the results. But no matter what the results have been, so far, these projects are of the greatest importance. They show that the community is assuming a responsibility toward the artist. Through them there may be a possibility of healing the breach between the artist and the public, a breach which has become distressingly evident in the contemporary period. It is to be hoped that the announced government plan to embellish federal buildings with paintings and sculptures will be carried through. In the end, of course, the scope and character of American mural art will depend on the architects. It cannot be said that the architects have covered themselves with glory in this field. With the lone exception of Henry Hobson Richardson their example has not been reassuring.

REGIONAL DEVELOPMENTS

One of the most interesting developments in recent years has been the growth of regional art groups devoted to exploring various local aspects of the American scene. Today there are several regional centers which have become important. Chicago has a strong group

Boston. This work, carried through in great haste by La Farge and his associates in 1876, remains on the whole the soundest mural decoration in this country. La Farge's painting in the Church of the Ascension, New York, is his best, and is one of the high points of American mural art, but since it is not an integral part of a decorative scheme it has less importance than the Boston work. Unlike his contemporaries and successors La Farge had not lost touch with the great decorative tradition in painting. Following Delacroix and the Venetians, he believed that mural painting should be fully realized and rich in color, and in spite of the insistence of most architects that the painting shall not break the plane of the wall, his seems the most healthy note in American mural art.

La Farge's work roused high hopes for the mural in this country, hopes which were meagerly realized by the work of a number of men at the Chicago World's Fair of 1893, the decorations in the Public Library in Boston, the Congressional Library in Washington, and other libraries, capitols and court houses. The works of Elihu Vedder, Kenyon Cox, Will H. Low, Abbott H. Thayer, Edwin H. Blashfield, Edward Simmons, Edwin H. Abbey, Siddons Mowbray, John Singer Sargent, J. W. Alexander, William De Leftwitch Dodge, Barry Faulkner and others offer nothing which reaches the standard set by La Farge. Arthur B. Davies' murals at Inter-

national House, New York, are interesting. Augustus Vincent Tack has done work which has the merit of personal research. But in general the mural painters of this country have depended on outworn formulas of the academic-popular type. Their work has been antiquarian and archaistic, echoing faintly the grand style of the Italian Renaissance which had been the ideal of La Farge.

American artists in recent years have given a good deal of thought to the problems of mural painting, that is, that the mural must be an integral part of the architectural scheme, that the color, the scale and the character of the painting must harmonize with the scale and character of the interior, have clearness of composition and carrying power, and a rhythmic order which leads the eye easily through the whole space. While they have not yet arrived at a thoroughly satisfactory mural art, they have brought the vitality and the restless movement of contemporary life to the walls of American buildings. Their work has put an end to meaningless antiquarianism in mural decoration.

An American artist who has given considerable thought to the problems of mural painting is Thomas Benton. A restless and versatile talent, Benton has developed from his earlier emphasis upon design to an absorption in subject matter almost as complete as Homer's. He is the creator of a characteristic style of mural painting which has influenced

of artists, Ivan LeLorraine Albright, Aaron Bohrod, Francis Chapin, Gustaf Dalstrom, Frances Foy, Ramon Shiva, William S. Schwartz, Frances Strain, Rudolph Weisenborn. In Cleveland an intelligent museum policy has encouraged local artists for many years. Henry G. Keller, one of the soundest artists of America, is the leader of this group, and there are such talented younger artists as Clarence H. Carter, Elizabeth Bart Gerald and Paul B. Travis. In Philadelphia there are Julius Bloch, Arthur Carles, Earl Horter, Hobson Pittman, Frances Speight. In Boston, Frank W. Benson, Oliver Chaffee, Charles Hopkinson, Molly Luce, Harley Perkins. At Cedar Rapids, Iowa, there is Grant Wood who records the scene of the Middle West, the rolling hills, the farms, the toil-hardened people, in a decorative style which has both topical interest and humor. In Detroit there are Jay Boorsma, John Carroll, Roger Davis, Zoltan Sepeshy, Jean Paul Slusser, Edgar Lewis Yeager. In Minneapolis, Dewey Albinson, Cameron Booth, Erle Loran, Glen Mitchell. In Taos and Santa Fe there are Joseph Bakos, Ernest L. Blumenschein, Andrew Dasburg, Randall Davey, Victor Higgins, Willard Nash, B. J. O. Nordfeldt, Olive Rush, Will Shuster and Theodore Van Solen. In San Francisco, Jane Berlandina, Charles D. Duncan, Lucien Labaudt and Otis Oldfield. In Los Angeles, Mabel Alvarez, Conrad Buff, Clarence Hinkle. In Seattle, Kenneth Callahan, Peter Marinus Camfferman, Ambrose Patterson. This list does no more than scratch the surface of regional developments. It is possible that in the next decade we may see the rise of numerous community centers which will challenge the leadership of great art capitals like New York.

WATROUS
CELEBRATION OF THE MASS
Collection the Artist

A brief summary of American painting since the Civil War can do little more than make note of main tendencies. It is obviously impossible to discuss individual contributions extensively, especially in the contemporary field. Among present-day painters not otherwise mentioned and whose work has value are the following: Edmund Archer, Milton Avery, Paul Bartlett, A. S. Baylinson, Gifford Beal, Reynolds Beal, Maurice Becker, Ben Benn, Theresa Bernstein, Virginia Berresford, Edward Biberman, Isabel Bishop, Lucile Blanch, Oscar Bluemner, Fega Blumberg, Jerome Blum, Homer Boss, Fiske Boyd, Robert Brackman, Simeon Braguin, Edward Bruce, Henri Burkhard, Paul Burlin, David Burliuk, Bryson Burroughs, Vincent Canadé, Jo Cantine, James Chapin, C. K. Chatterton, Nicolai Cikovsky, Konrad Cramer, Florence Ballin Cramer, James E. Davis, Boris Deutsch, Joseph De Martini, Frank Di Gioia, Nathaniel Dirk, Thomas Donnelly, Stuart Edie, Stephen Etnier, Philip Evergood, Lauren Ford, Josef Foshko, Karl Free, Emil Ganso, Walter Gay, Wood Gaylor, Edwin Booth Grossman, Bernar Gussow, Robert Hallowell, Leon Hartl, Bertram Hartman, Harry Hering, Eugene Higgins, Hilaire Hiler, Emil Holzhauer, Gerrit Hondius, Isabella Howland, Herminie Kleinert, Georgina Klitgaard, Kai Klitgaard, Benjamin Kopman, Leon Kroll, Edward Laning, Sidney Laufman, Doris Lee, A. F. Levinson, Hayley Lever, Jonas Lie, William Littlefield, Eugene MacCown, Gus Mager, Peppino Mangravite, Jan Matulka, Paul R. Meltsner, Ross Moffett, Hermon More, Archibald J. Motley, Kimon Nicolaides, William C. Palmer, Waldo Peirce, Robert Philipp, Marjorie Phillips, Charles Prendergast, Misha Reznikoff, Louis Ritman, Caroline Speare Rohland, Paul Rohland, Umberto Romano, Charles Rosen, William Sanger, Saul, Saul Schary, William Schulhoff, Simka Simkhovitch, Judson Smith, Moses Soyer, Raphael Soyer, Carl Sprinchorn, Albert Sterner, Mark Tobey, Bradley Walker Tomlin, Herman Trunk, William von Schlegell, Nan Watson, Harold Weston, Warren Wheelock, William Yarrow.

KELLER
STORM-FRIGHTENED ANIMALS UNDER THE BIG HORSE TENT
Collection the Artist

· 49 ·

SHAHN
PROJECT FOR A MURAL

Photo by Walker Evans

SLOAN
SCULPTURE IN THE PARK (Etching)

Kraushaar Art Galleries, New York

WOOD
AMERICAN GOTHIC

The Art Institute of Chicago

BEAL
SEAGULLS

Kraushaar Art Galleries, New York

II. American Sculpture Since the Civil War

By HOLGER CAHILL

SCULPTURE IN general divides into two broad classifications, the relief and sculpture in the round. Aside from Augustus Saint-Gaudens few American sculptors have produced important work in relief. The types of sculpture may be divided, roughly, into the portrait, the figure, the civic or commemorative monument, and architectural sculpture. From the time of William Rush and John Frazee many American sculptors have produced excellent work in portraits and single figures. Except for the work of the provincial carvers there was very little architectural sculpture in this country up to the close of the Civil War. After the Civil War there was a great demand for monuments, but until John Quincy Adams Ward produced his *General Thomas* (1878) and Augustus Saint-Gaudens his *Farragut* (1881), the results were not very impressive.

In the decade after the close of the Civil War, American sculpture offered little but mediocre Italianate imitations. The professional sculptors of the period were busied with smooth futilities in white marble, as they had been since the 1830's. Divorced from the life of their country and even from their medium of expression (most of them lived in Italy and had their work carried out by stone cutters) they lingered in a pseudo-classic twilight. Their ideal of style was the pale refinement of Canova and Thorwaldsen; their ideal of beauty a sentimentalized version of the Venus of Medici.

Far more interesting than the professional sculpture was the work of craftsmen, workers in metal, stone and wood, who carved and modeled figureheads, gravestones, and decorations for houses, shops and ships. Most of these craftsmen were unsophisticated and had no idea that they were creating art, but among them were some master carvers. Their work may still be seen in the occasional cigar store Indians, lawn figures and weather-vanes in out-of-the-way villages and in the collections of historical societies. While the tradition of these folk artists was rapidly dying out at the close of the Civil War many of them were still producing decorative sculpture admirable for fitness, simplicity and just proportion, and one of them, John Bellamy, last of the figurehead carvers, was employed in the navy yard at Portsmouth, N. H.

A reaction against the artificialities of the mid-century Italianate style appears in the work of John Rogers, Henry Kirke Brown, and John Quincy Adams Ward. As a young man Rogers became discouraged with the milky perfections of the pseudo-classic and in the 1860's began modeling small groups of figures, the "Rogers groups" which had an immense popularity in their day. Sidney Lanier, the poet, called him the "brightest example of genius in the art yet afforded by our country." However, Rogers' work cannot be called sculpture. It is illustration carried out in the materials of sculpture, but it has a good deal of humor and homely sentiment (*Union Refugees*). Henry Kirke Brown studied four years in Italy, but after he returned to this country he abandoned the marble visions of his apprentice years and went to live among the Indians. A return to the native American realistic tradition of Rush and Frazee appears in his work, the best of which is the equestrian *Washington* in Union Square, New York, on which his pupil, Ward, worked with him. Frederick Remington's sculptured illustrations of cowboy life are not unlike the Rogers' groups, but they have much more vitality. Remington's work is not conceived in the terms of sculpture, but it is lively and shows a great deal of skill in suggesting spirited movement (*Broncho Buster*).

John Quincy Adams Ward was an American-trained sculptor. He was a thorough craftsman who knew how to model, carve, and cast. His work is akin to that of Brown, but shows more understanding of the qualities of naturalistic form, a better feeling for mass, and a more intense study of character. Ward had Homer's interest in subject and something of Eakins' realistic probity. In his early work he was perhaps too faithful to the small detail, but even in his accumulation of fact there is always seriousness and honest, simple strength. After the insipid suavities of the Italian-trained sculptors the forthright realism of his *Henry Ward Beecher*

ANONYMOUS
NEW ENGLAND WEATHER-VANE

Private Collection

ment, the *Alexander Hamilton* in Boston, is disappointing, but he was one of the "originals" of American art, a colorful character in a drab period.

The Centennial Exposition in Philadelphia in 1876 marks a turning point in American sculpture. The Exposition itself had little to do with the change. It simply announced the fact that the more advanced of the Europe-trained sculptors were turning from the cold pseudo-classicism of Rome to the livelier romanticism of Paris. Two of the most brilliant of the Paris-trained men, Olin Levi Warner and Augustus Saint-Gaudens, were working in America by 1876. Both had studied at the *Ecole des Beaux Arts*. While their teacher, Jouffroy, was one of the more conservative exponents

Rimmer, physician, painter, sculptor, and teacher of anatomy. Rimmer seems to have learned all he knew about sculpture from engravings of the work of Michelangelo and from a few casts of the antique. While his work has power and expressiveness, it is over-modeled and over-anatomical. His one public monu-

(Brooklyn) strikes a vigorous and wholesome note. As his work progressed it gained in breadth, the modeling became more flexible and expressive, the feeling for form more sensitive. In his heroic figure of *Washington* which stands before the Sub-Treasury Building in New York, Ward achieved a breadth and monumentality far above the general run of American sculpture of the nineteenth century.

In Ward's early years it was difficult for sculptors to get the right kind of training in this country—even more difficult than it was for the painters. Up to the middle seventies it was impossible to find art classes that worked from the nude model. A mid-nineteenth century sculptor who might have done more consistently good work if he had had better opportunities for study was William

but his first important work was the *Farragut* monument in Madison Square, New York. With this monument Saint-Gaudens became the leading American sculptor of his time. The *Farragut* is a thoroughly sound work, excellent in characterization, well constructed and well placed. It set a new standard for American monumental sculpture. Saint-Gaudens' *Lincoln,* in Lincoln Park, Chicago (1887), caught the popular imagination and was hailed as the greatest portrait statue in the United States. The *Lincoln* shows Saint-Gaudens' reserved realism, his impressionistic handling of surfaces enlivened with a play of light and shade (products of his French training) and something of his "idealizing tendency." This idealizing tendency, a heritage of pseudo-classicism on one side

and of the pervasive American tradition of "seeing beautifully" on the other, comes out more strongly in the women's portraits and in the relief portraits of children. *The Peace of God* (Adams Memorial, Washington, D. C., 1891) is probably Saint-Gaudens' best work. This has sometimes been called the greatest sculpture produced in this country. It is without question a fine work, handled with breadth and simplicity and with a feeling for monumentality. The figure is beautifully placed, bronze against stone, with the contrast of the figure against the rectangles of base and background. In the *Shaw Memorial* in Boston, a work in high relief, there is an interesting handling of rhythmic movement and the grouping of many figures. Beside the *Farragut,* the *Lincoln,* the

of the new ideas, through him they came into contact with the work of François Rude (1784-1855), Antoine Louis Barye (1795-1875) and Jean-Baptiste Carpeaux (1827-1875), men who had turned from pseudo-classicism to a new interpretation of rococo, baroque and Renaissance sculpture. The French movement was romantic and realistic. It emphasized picturesqueness, movement in surface and silhouette, animation, expressiveness, and a more naturalistic treatment of the nude. Warner, who studied with Jouffroy and worked for a time in the studio of Carpeaux, was a splendid technician who never broke completely with the pseudo-classic ideas which had influenced him in his youth. His work has clarity, sensitive modeling, and a good deal of grace and charm.

Augustus Saint-Gaudens was apprenticed to a cameo cutter at the age of thirteen, and in this early training developed the skill in low relief which made him the American master in this field. He studied at Cooper Union and the National Academy of Design in New York before he went to Paris, returning to this country in 1875. In 1876 he worked under John La Farge on the decoration of Trinity Church in Boston,

SAINT-GAUDENS
ROBERT LOUIS STEVENSON
The Augustus Saint-Gaudens Memorial, Cornish, N. H.

Grey Barnard. He studied at the Chicago Art Institute and in Paris under Carlier, and felt the influence of Rodin. The Rodin influence, however, did little more than turn his attention to Michelangelo. A man of great energy and a born carver, Barnard had produced his heroic *Two Natures* (Metropolitan Museum) before he was twenty-three years old. When his work was shown in Paris in 1894 it won immediate success. Great things were prophesied for him. He has not lived up to this early promise, though he is an artist of rich endowment, and is certainly the outstanding sculptor of the older generation in this country. Barnard loves the colossal and has devoted most of his life to thinking great thoughts in stone. His utterance

BARNARD
ABRAHAM LINCOLN
Photo Perry
Lytle Park, Cincinnati

Shaw Memorial and the *Adams Memorial,* the best work of Saint-Gaudens is in his low reliefs (*Robert Louis Stevenson*). Saint-Gaudens' conception of sculpture was at times over-pictorial, as in the *General Sherman,* New York, and his interest in liveliness of surface (*Amor Caritas,* Metropolitan Museum) sometimes made him carry to extremes the French drapery formulas. While his work is not conspicuous for originality, it has strength, style, and dignity, and the charm of poetic sentiment.

There is not much to fire the imagination in the works of Saint-Gaudens' followers in popularity, Herbert Adams, Clement John Barnhorn, Paul W. Bartlett, Karl Bitter, Gutzon Borglum, Solon Borglum, John Boyle, Victor D. Brenner, Cyrus E. Dallin, John Donoghue, John Flanagan, Charles Grafly, Charles Keck, Isidore Konti, Augustus Lukeman, Hermon McNeil, Philip Martiny, Frederick MacMonnies, Charles Henry Niehaus, Attilio Piccirilli, A. Phimister Proctor, J. Massey Rhind, F. G. R. Roth, Frederick Ruckstull, Lorado Taft, A. W. Weinman, and others. Craftsmen of sound training, most of them, eclectic and industrious talents, interested in surfaces and in impressionistic handling that runs to the pictorial and photographic, they have produced portraits and decorative and monumental sculpture of an academic-popular type.

Daniel Chester French, pupil of Rimmer in Boston, Ward in New York, and Thomas Ball in Florence, produced some work of dignity and simplicity, but in general he leaves much to be desired. His most popular work is probably *Death and the Sculptor,* (Milmore Memorial, Forest Hills Cemetery, Boston), and his most impressive, the *Lincoln* of the Lincoln Memorial in Washington, D. C. Frederick MacMonnies is an able technician with too emphatic an insistence upon the clay modeler's virtuosity. His cleverness as a modeler is evident in such a figure as the *Nathan Hale* in City Hall Park, New York, but his work, with its restless, unresolved movement, is rather empty and unconvincing. Charles Grafly was one of the best academic portrait sculptors. Victor D. Brenner was a talented medallist.

The promise of a sounder realism and a more intelligent understanding of the tradition of baroque and Renaissance sculpture appears in the work of George

is cryptic, and he shows a tendency to lose himself in gargantuan conceptions, but he has both imaginative force and originality and a better feeling for mass than any other sculptor of his generation. His best work is probably the *Lincoln,* a powerful, homely conception, and by all odds the best monument to Lincoln yet produced. Other fine single figures are *The Hewer* (Cairo, Ill.) and *Rising Woman* (Pocantico Hills, N. Y.). The figures at the Pennsylvania State Capitol at Harrisburg are excellent, but the organization of such large groups of free-standing figures is a very difficult problem and Barnard has not completely solved it in this instance. For the past sixteen years he has been working on a colossal monument to the dead in the World War, a group of fifty-three heroic figures grouped on two sides of a great arch. The model for this was completed in 1933. Any estimate of this extraordinary undertaking must wait until it is carried out in stone. Like John La Farge and Arthur B. Davies, Barnard is a profound student of art, and a connoisseur of the sculpture of the Middle Ages. He formed the splendid collection of medieval sculpture known as The Cloisters, now owned by the Metropolitan Museum, New York.

American sculpture in the past twenty years has been turning away from its concern with surface and silhouette, its anatomical realism and its idealizing tendencies to a renewed interest in the architectonic. This change has been brought about by the ideas and movements which were discussed in the article on modernism in painting. American sculptors today are in a very different position from that of the men of the sixties and seventies. They now have unprecedented opportunities for study. Not only are there excellent schools in this country, but museums of art and archæology today have built up sculpture collections of great range and variety. In addition to this illustrations and photographs, which are a far more exact record of sculpture than they are of painting, make it possible for the sculptor to study the art of all countries and periods.

This new wealth of facts has been used by different sculptors in different ways. With some it has led to a hollow and meaningless eclecticism. With others it has meant a chance to study the basic problems of sculpture in all ages, and these artists have turned away from the impressionistic methods of the nineteenth century. They have concentrated their attention on the architectural foundations of sculpture, on rhythm, mass, organic structure, unity of space, rhythmic relation of mass and space, and on

EPSTEIN
MADONNA AND CHILD

simplifications that tend toward the abstract and the primitive. They have revived the idea implicit in all good sculpture, and explicitly stated by Michelangelo, of a collaboration between the sculptor and his material.

The sculptor's materials impose upon him certain limitations but these very limitations may be made to enhance the esthetic quality of his work. He can take advantage of the very hardness and resistance of stone, its weight, grain and color. The harder materials are suited to concepts that suggest gravity, calmness, monumentality. They call for a method of working in broad planes that take the light evenly. Wood, which carves easily, has its own beauty of grain and texture and is suited to a suave treatment or to elaborate surfaces. The hard flowing surfaces of metal are ideally suited to naturalistic treatment. They may be made to reproduce all the nuances of the clay-modeler's technique

—the sudden transitions of crest and hollow and the individual peculiarities of form that make for expressiveness and character. Metal surfaces may be roughened to make a dramatic interplay of light and shade, polished to reflect light, or given a patina which enhances warmth and variety of surface.

The Italianate sculptors of the mid-century were clay modelers whose work was cast in plaster, pointed-up, and carved in marble. Most of the Paris-trained men of the seventies, eighties and nineties were modelers whose final medium was bronze. In the past thirty years most of the leading American sculptors have been carvers as well as modelers. Direct carving in hard stone makes for concentration on mass and geometric form rather than on lively surfaces or naturalistic treatment, and for this reason it has been a most beneficial discipline for American sculptors. Of the generation now in maturity such

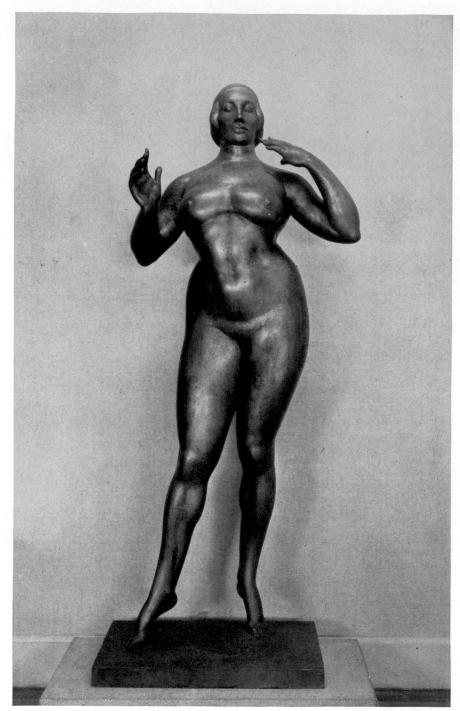

LACHAISE
FIGURE OF A WOMAN   Collection John A. Dunbar, New York

in Paris. For the past thirty years he has lived in America. He believes that "the soil most fertile for the continuity of art—is here." Lachaise is a sculptor of great originality and an accomplished technician. In his concern with rhythmic movement and warm treatment of surfaces he is an inheritor of the best elements in the baroque tradition of French sculpture. A direct carver as well as a modeler, he has a thorough knowledge of the possibilities and limitations of his materials. He has found very interesting solutions for the problem of relating masses in continuous rhythm, and achieves a splendor of formal relation, especially in the handling of round forms. In his *Figure of a Woman* there is an elegance of posture that is essentially baroque, and an elevation and plenitude of form. While

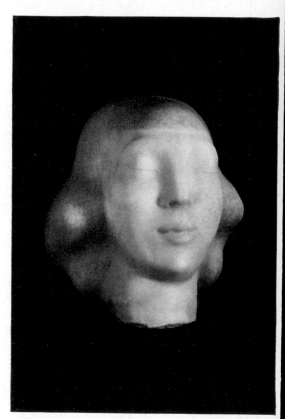

LACHAISE   Private Collection
WOMAN'S HEAD

sculptors as Jacob Epstein, William Zorach, Gaston Lachaise, Maurice Sterne, Elie Nadelman, Robert Laurent, and John Storrs have done important work in direct carving.

Of contemporary American sculptors the most widely known is Jacob Epstein, an expatriate who lives in London. Epstein studied in New York and at the *Ecole des Beaux Arts* and the Julian Academy in Paris before he went to England. In direct carving he has done architectural and monumental sculpture of highly individual quality but he is primarily a modeler. "I try to express the character of what I am depicting," Epstein has said of his work. In his portraits he is concerned with the expressiveness which comes from accenting the forms which give unique character

to a face, and with roughened surfaces which intensify character and which are also capable of being interesting in themselves. His work has an autographic quality, a feeling of the process of making and of the materials in which he works. In bronze he gets a dramatic contrast of light and shade in broken surfaces, and an effect of spontaneity and nervous force. In stone he emphasizes the great planes rather than individual variations and achieves an effect of brooding intensity. Epstein is a talent of the romantic type. He is without question one of the best portrait sculptors of the contemporary period. His art has an aliveness and emotional power which is at times almost savage.

Gaston Lachaise was born in France and studied at the *Ecole des Beaux Arts*

Lachaise's work has the decorative quality which lends itself to architecture, his best work has been in portraits and single figures.

William Zorach studied at the National Academy of Design in New York, and in Paris. He is primarily a direct carver though he is also an excellent modeler. More than most contemporaries Zorach is concerned with the architectural foundations of sculpture and with a study of geometric form, the relation of curved and angular, mound and hollow, the thrust and counterthrust of planes that define and relate masses. He is more concerned with rhythmic order and movement of mass than with the handling of surface and silhouette. One feels in his work a deep interest in the architecture of forms revolving around a central axis. His work has a profoundly stirring emotional quality, sincerity and depth, and a harmony between spontaneity and firmly ordered design. Such sculptures as *Mother and Child,* the torso in the Whitney Museum of American Art in New York, and his recent studies of animals are powerful examples of the "organization of stone form as a symbol of life," one of the best definitions of the ideals of the direct carver.*

Maurice Sterne, who studied at Cooper Union and at the National Academy of Design, works in large simplified forms handled with a clear understanding of the interplay of mass and space. His work has the austere selection, the feeling for scale, and something of the

* Quoted from *The Meaning of Modern Sculpture* by R. H. Wilenski.

ZORACH
CAT

Private Collection, New York

large spirit of the classic. In such works as the *Rogers Kennedy Memorial* he achieves a monumentality which is impressive. An interpretation of classic elegance and grace which makes the work of contemporary academic classi-

cists and the mid-century Italianates look very commonplace is that of Elie Nadelman. *Head in Marble* is an example of his early work. He has not shown for many years and appears to be working toward a completely different style. Robert Laurent is one of the best direct carvers among contemporary sculptors. He is a stylist with a fine sense of linear continuity, and handles decorative form with distinction. In alabaster he achieves particularly happy effects and his carvings of plant forms in wood have sensitiveness, suavity and grace.

An interesting development in contemporary sculpture is the art of Carl Walters who uses pottery fired at high temperatures as freely as the average sculptor uses clay. He has achieved an extraordinary mastery of the ceramic technique and gets very good effects with polychrome. John Storrs is concerned with architectonic structure and geometric form and has produced excellent architectural sculpture. He is one of the few Americans who have experimented with purely abstract forms. An important pioneer in abstract sculpture is Alexander Archipenko, a Russian who now lives in America. Archipenko is a clever designer, and his work with its highly polished surfaces has something of the feeling of machine design. The work of Hunt Diederich has decorative quality and an arbitrary simplification which is related to heraldic design. His almost exclusive concern with the ornamental has narrowed the scope of a genuine talent. Alfeo Faggi is a stylist and one of the few modern sculptors who have tried to convey religious feeling.

Paul Manship has derived from Renaissance, archaic and Oriental sculpture a suave form and a decorative handling of silhouette and drapery, though he has little feeling for mass. His technical proficiency is remarkable but he lacks originality and creative force. He is the

ZORACH
MOTHER AND CHILD

The Downtown Gallery, New York

· 57 ·

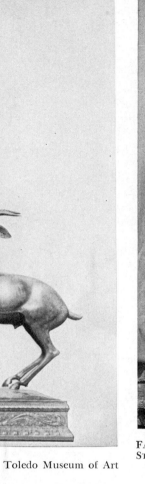

MANSHIP
DANCER AND GAZELLES

Toledo Museum of Art

FAGGI
ST. FRANCIS

Museum of New Mexico,
Santa Fe

DIEDERICH
JOCKEY

The Newark Museum

LEE
VOLUPTE

The Brooklyn Museum

· 58 ·

YOUNG
CHISELER

Collection the Artist

HUNTINGTON
JOAN OF ARC

Photo Juley
Riverside Drive, New York

leading adept of the cult of archaistic prettiness fostered by the American Academy in Rome, and his work brings up the question of the wide-ranging eclecticism made possible by modern archæological research. His archaistic-academic-popular style has enormous prestige with the architects. It seems destined to dominate American architectural and monumental sculpture in this generation just as the style of Daniel Chester French was dominant in the last generation.

Among the older contemporaries Mahonri Young has produced excellent realistic figures of laborers; Jo Davidson's contribution is in his portraits of outstanding personalities of our time; Arthur Lee has a fine understanding of the classic and is a sensitive modeler; Warren Wheelock has a feeling for decorative simplification and is well-known both as sculptor and painter; Edward McCartan is an excellent technician with a feeling for surfaces; James Earle Fraser has something of the poetry of Saint-Gaudens but not his strength;

John Gregory is a stylist tending to the lyrical and the archaic; Robert I. Aitken is an eclectic and accomplished technician; the late Charles Cary Rumsey produced some work which shows a good feeling for mass. Others who may be mentioned are Chester Beach, Salvatore Bilotti, A. Stirling Calder, Allan Clark, Rudolph Evans, John Flanagan, Leo Friedlander, Sherry Fry, Trygve Hammer, Herbert Haseltine, Cecil Howard, C. P. Jennewein, Charles Keck, Mario Korbel, Lee Lawrie, Leo Lentelli, B. Lovet-Lorski, Attilio Piccirilli, Albin Polasek.

A number of women sculptors have done good work: Sonia Brown, Betty Burroughs, Gladys Caldwell, Louise Cross, Abastenia St. Leger Eberle, Harriet Frishmuth, Eugenie Gershoy, Anna Glenny, Minna Harkavy, Malvina Hoffman, Anna V. Hyatt Huntington, Evelyn B. Longman, Gwen Lux, Renée Prahar, Hélène Sardeau, Janet Scudder, Eugenie F. Shonnard, Marion Walton, Ann Weaver, Gertrude V. Whitney. Perhaps the most promising of the younger women sculptors is Concetta Scaravagli-

one, whose work has largeness of scale and a feeling for full, round forms.

Outstanding among the younger sculptors are Ahron Ben-Shmuel, a fine carver and a stylist who tends to the primitive; Harold Cash, who is interested in design and expression; Alexander Calder, who appears to be concerned with what the Germans call sculpture-in-itself; Duncan Ferguson whose work has something of the contained emotional quality of Oriental sculpture; Reuben Nakian, one of the most talented of the younger men, a gifted carver and modeler who is bringing a new realism into portrait sculpture; Isamu Noguchi, an experimenter interested in abstraction. Other younger sculptors are: Albino Cavallito, Samuel Cashwan, Gaetano Cecere, Wharton Esherick, Mitchell Fields, Paul Fiene, John B. Flannagan, Vincent Glinsky, Aaron J. Goodelman, Chaim Gross, Milton Horn, James House, Jr., Oronzio Maldarelli, Hugo Robus, Antonio Salemme, Victor Salvatore, Cesare Stea, Dudley Vail Talcott, Polygnotos Vagis, Heinz Warneke, Wheeler Williams.

WALTERS
BULL

Whitney Museum of American Art

CALDER
MOBILE

Collection the Artist

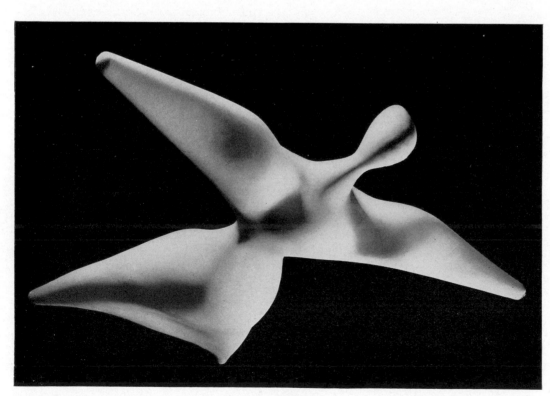

NOGUCHI
MISS EXPANDING UNIVERSE

Collection the Artist

NAKIAN   The Downtown
ALEXANDER BROOK   Gallery, New York

STERNE   Rogers-Kennedy Memorial, Worcester, Mass.
MONUMENT TO THE EARLY SETTLERS

NADELMAN   Collection Mme. Helena
HEAD IN MARBLE   Rubinstein, New York

STORRS   Collection William Bullitt,
ABSTRACT SCULPTURE   Philadelphia

WHEELOCK   Collection the Artist
THE EMBRACE

LAURENT
SEATED FIGURE

Collection John A. Dunbar, New York

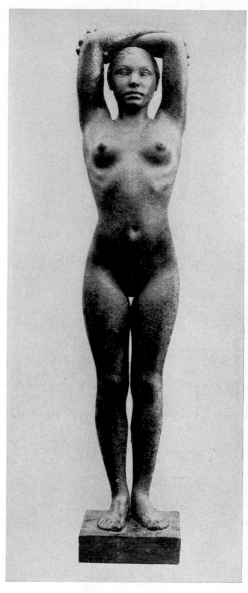

CASH
STANDING FIGURE

Collection the Artist

BEN-SHMUEL
SEATED WOMAN

Museum of Modern Art,
New York

III. Architecture

I. HENRY HOBSON RICHARDSON: THE DEVELOPMENT OF THE SKYSCRAPER

BY HENRY-RUSSELL HITCHCOCK, JR.

THE CIVIL WAR was followed in the North by a building boom which lasted until the panic of 1873. This boom was singularly unproductive of good architecture. Even before the Civil War the strong Greek tradition of the 1830's had been replaced by a welter of feeble imitations of current European manners of building. After the Civil War no single national tradition of style was left with which to work. Architects and builders followed in their busy practice the fashions of London and Paris as they were transmitted across the Atlantic by woodcuts in the English magazines.

The rather gaudy Renaissance and Baroque splendors of the Second Empire provided models for public buildings such as the State, War and Navy Department in Washington by Mullet. Post offices and city halls throughout the country imitated crudely in granite the superimposed orders of pilasters and columns of the Tuileries. The mansard roof—a seventeenth century invention—was the symbol of modernity for all sorts of buildings.

Equally important was the influence of the English Victorian Gothic which dominated in ecclesiastical and educational architecture in America. In domestic design it divided the field with the French style. An amusing instance of the equal dominance of the two manners is to be seen in two buildings at the Worcester Institute of Technology, both by Elbridge Boyden, built side by side in 1866. One is of brick in the mansard-roofed French manner, and the other of granite with the pointed arches and pointed roofs of the Victorian Gothic. The second is the better of the two.

Generally speaking, the best talent and the best thought of the day were given to the Victorian Gothic. The old railroad station in Worcester, by Ware & Van Brunt is one of the best works of the early seventies. William A. Potter's South Congregational Church in Springfield, Mass., is not unworthy of comparison with the English work of Butterfield and Street which it imitates. The Gothic houses were not very Gothic but they were generally better planned than the mansarded mansions. The vast majority of building of the

time, however, particularly that produced by contractors and builders without architectural advice, defies classification. The hangover of the Romantic manners of the forties and fifties, the muddle of French and English and even German motifs produced a chaos of architectural design which was particularly marked in city houses and commercial buildings.

The career of Richardson, the greatest American architect and perhaps the greatest American artist of the later nineteenth century, began in this post-Civil War period of chaos. Returning in 1865 from a thorough training at the *Ecole des Beaux Arts* in Paris, by 1870 he had developed his personal style, not on what he had known in Paris or what was being done around him. He formed it, rather, on what he found in early nineteenth century books of medieval archæology and on the best contemporary English work in the magazines. His very first buildings were not distinguished. In the early seventies he began to design with real power and originality, drawing his inspiration particularly from the Romanesque style, about which he then knew very little. His Hampden County Court House was begun in 1871. With its Italian medieval tower, and its

great granite arches, its simple rectangular windows and high dormers, this was his first fine building. The simplicity, the sense of masonry, the vigorous and original proportions are all more splendidly manifest in it than in Trinity Church, which was begun in Boston the following year and established his reputation. Another good early building was the Cheney Building (1875), in Hartford, now Brown, Thompson & Company, in which he applied his individual style of design to a commercial structure. Even in these early buildings Richardson was able to surpass most of his European contemporaries in vigor and integrity of design.

The period of Richardson's maturity began in 1878 with the building of Sever Hall at Harvard. In its simple brickwork, carefully studied masses and well-designed ornament, there is nothing specifically Romanesque; rather, there are all the marks of a fully developed personal style. More Romanesque, perhaps, is his Quincy Library of 1881. It is admirably planned and most originally composed on lines of functional asymmetry. It is the best of a series of libraries which he built in New England. Also in 1881 he began a series of rail-

HENRY HOBSON RICHARDSON: CRANE MEMORIAL LIBRARY   Quincy, Mass., 1881-82

HENRY HOBSON RICHARDSON: Stoughton House
Cambridge, Mass., 1882
Photo Berenice Abbott

road stations for the Boston & Albany Railroad. His first and best, at Auburndale, was the simplest possible essay in massive masonry, with heavy timber porches at the entrance and along the tracks. During the same period he developed a new type of wooden house, picturesque in massing and free in planning. This is best represented in the Stoughton House in Cambridge, Mass. The simplicity of Richardson's shingle-covered houses is in striking contrast to the confused and fantastic Queen Anne detail used by his best American contemporaries and even by his sometime pupils, McKim and White.

Before his death in 1886 Richardson had become the leading architect of the country and one of the busiest. In the gray granite Glessner House in Chicago, completed after his death, he avoided the over-monumental character of most of his masonry houses. The main rooms of the house face an inner court, away from the street, a plan admirably adapted to a corner lot. In the Marshall Field Wholesale Store (1886) in the same city, he simplified and perfected the scheme of monumental masonry design initiated in the Cheney Building.

Richardson's influence and following from the mid-seventies until 1893 was the greatest in the country. Unfortunately his pupils and imitators rarely caught the significant informing simplicity and unified composition of his best work.

The "Richardsonian" was chiefly a semi-archæological and chaotically picturesque Romanesque revival. Rock-faced brownstone masonry, low, broad arches, round towers, scrawling ornament were all most American architects could see in his work. The corruption of his style prepared the way for a sharp reaction toward formal Renaissance principles of design, which was led by McKim, Mead & White in the mid-eighties.

This decade was the period not only of the Romanesque and the American version of the Queen Anne—and the resultant reaction against both; it was the decade also in which the development of the skyscraper culminated. Skyscraper construction is not a matter of height (indeed, it is used today in many low buildings), it is a way of building with a metal skeleton, similar to wood frame construction. It is the antithesis of masonry construction, in use since the Pyramids. The skyscraper is a product of technical advances along several lines. In 1848 cast iron, not only for interior supports but even for facades, was introduced in New York by Bogardus. In the fifties, metal skeleton construction began gradually to replace masonry bearing walls. With the introduction of the elevator in 1868, buildings higher than six stories became convenient and acceptable.

In the Home Insurance Building, begun in Chicago in 1884, Major Jenney provided a metal skeleton which carried all the interior weight of the building and largely carried the weight of the masonry exterior walls as well. In the Tacoma Building (1887) in Chicago by Holabird & Roche the weight of the exterior sheathing was entirely transferred to the interior metal skeleton, and true skyscraper construction came into existence. Each building has a claim to being the first skyscraper. At the same time Burnham & Root were making improvements in the foundations of all types of tall buildings, and steel was gradually being substituted for cast and wrought iron.

Although the technical development of the skyscraper was complete by 1890, skyscraper design was characterless. It echoed the same Romanesque and Renaissance motifs then fashionable for smaller buildings. Only the Tacoma Building showed the new openness which skeleton construction made possible and logical.

It was left to Louis Sullivan in the nineties to devise original formulas of design adapted to tall buildings and expressive of the underlying skeleton. In the late eighties Sullivan had been one of the few to apply Richardson's principles of masonry design with success in the Auditorium Building in Chicago. When he began to use skyscraper construction in the Wainright Building in St. Louis in 1890, he omitted almost entirely from its exterior sheathing the arches and other traditional features of masonry design, except the cornice. In order to emphasize the height he introduced extra vertical members between the supporting piers from the base of the building to the cornice. This scheme, with two or three windows to a bay and no marked differentiation in the external appearance between the supporting piers and the extra verticals, has remained the characteristic type of non-traditional skyscraper design down to the present day. Although Sullivan designed several buildings in Chicago, New York and Buffalo similar to the Wainright Building, he was not long satisfied to cling to the windows of the ordinary vertical shape. During the nineties he worked out a second and more logical type of design in which the windows were horizontal and filled the whole width of the bay. At the same time he reduced the sheathing of the piers and floor lines to a minimum so that the surface appearance of the building no longer suggested a solid wall or a row of closely set piers, but rather a glazed cage with the vertical and horizontal bars lightly covered with terra-cotta. The great example of this type of design is the Schlesinger-Mayer Build-

HENRY HOBSON RICHARDSON: Marshall Field Wholesale Store   Chicago, 1886

HENRY HOBSON RICHARDSON: Harrison Avenue, Boston, 1886
Ames Building

BURNHAM & ROOT: Monadnock Building   Chicago, 1891

LOUIS HENRY SULLIVAN: Schlesinger-Mayer Building   Chicago, 1899

ing (1899) in Chicago, now Carson, Pirie & Scott.

These two types of design, the vertical and the horizontal, established by Sullivan in the nineties, are still the most successful in giving architectural character to the skyscraper. Among the skyscrapers built in the last few years, Raymond Hood's Daily News Building, Shreve, Lamb & Harmon's Empire State Building, and the Rockefeller Center Tower by Hood, Harrison and others, are perhaps the best examples of the vertical type. They are enormously taller than the Wainright Building, are without its traditional cornice and are intended to be seen like towers from all sides, yet they are essentially the same in principle of design. Of the horizontal type the latest examples are Hood's McGraw-Hill Building (1932) in New York, and Howe & Lescaze's Philadelphia Savings Fund Society Building (1932) in Philadelphia.

In the West, Sullivan's non-traditional skyscraper designs were influential from the first. In the East his leading contemporaries sought to apply to the skyscraper the academic Classical type of design then dominant in other fields. The academic prejudice demanded that the walls, although supported by an interior skeleton, should look like solid supporting masonry cut up by isolated windows of traditional vertical shape. For embellishment the lower stories were given some elaborate treatment such as a colonnade, which was usually repeated with slight modification on the top stories beneath a large and complicated projecting cornice. The shaft of the building between the embellished top and bottom was, of course, less richly decorated. One of the best and earliest of the skyscraper towers was the Metropolitan Life Insurance Building in New York by LeBrun (1906). This was in the form of an Italian campanile with a pointed top, the whole enormously enlarged and pierced with large, coupled windows. Unfortunately this relatively intelligent scheme was rarely imitated. The later New York Municipal Building by McKim, Mead & White (1912) was interesting in its adaptation to a difficult site but its appeal was chiefly in the rather frivolous colonnaded and turreted superstructure above the cornice. This type of purely decorative culmination has been very popular.

On the Woolworth Building in New York (1911-1913) Cass Gilbert substituted for the conventional embellishment of Classical or Renaissance inspiration an overlay of Gothic motifs in which the vertical was persistently stressed and the decorative treatment of the top better co-ordinated with the rest of the design.

RAYMOND HOOD: DAILY NEWS BUILDING New York, 1930

In the last thirty years almost every sort of archæological embellishment has been occasionally used.

As late as 1922 Hood's winning design in the Chicago Tribune Tower competition, in which all academic variants of the skyscraper formula were offered, was still very Gothic. Saarinen's design, which was generally admired and very influential, offered no important alternative beyond the substitution of stylized and simplified medieval detail for the more archæological sort and the avoidance of an ornamental top.

Before 1929 the last important modification of the skyscraper formula was brought about by the zoning law in New York, which required that build-ings reaching a certain height be stepped back from the street line. This resulted in a new interest in stepped and pyramidal massing. The zoning law only slightly overcame the practical difficulties of lost daylight and congestion which the spread of the skyscraper had made so serious. The increasing omission of cornices and the substitution of freer and better scaled ornament on the new silhouette achieved no new style but was merely a superficial modification of the original academic scheme with its simulated masonry walls. Ralph Walker's Telephone Building (1925) in New York, for example, obtains its effect by suggesting a medieval fortress and is completely opposed in almost every respect to the fine early skyscrapers by Sullivan.

Skyscraper architects are now returning to the simpler and more effective formulas of Sullivan. This is not so much in emulation of his early skyscrapers, swallowed up among taller buildings and largely forgotten, as because of the influence of twentieth century European architecture.

The nineteenth century is notable in American architecture for the genius of Henry Hobson Richardson, and because it contributed to world architecture an entirely new form of building which is typically American—the skyscraper.

II. ACADEMIC REVIVALISM
By Henry-Russell Hitchcock, Jr.

THE GREAT architectural achievements of the last quarter of the nineteenth century in America were Richardson's and Sullivan's. But the general tendency was in opposition to them and to the spirit of original creation they represented. On the death of Richardson in 1886 he was hailed by his contemporaries as a very great architect but not for those qualities which seem particularly admirable today. They considered him a revivalist, one of the first to use photographic documents to imitate buildings of the past. To them, following him meant following a Romanesque or Byzantine revival. The more sophisticated went a step further and applied the same technique to the styles of later centuries.

The particular sort of revivalism which absorbed the energies of most of the leaders of American architecture after Richardson's death was not a European importation, but a product of local conditions. Nationalism turned attention to the eighteenth century Colonial and the style of the Early Republic, much as Europe earlier had turned to the Gothic. The forms of the Romanesque and Gothic seemed unsuited to modern conditions, whereas the academic tradition (of which the Colonial was a part) appeared adaptable. Americans felt that they were to have a period of world hegemony comparable to that of France under Louis XIV; and like the French they turned to Italy and to the Classical past. It was surprisingly easy for these late nineteenth century revivalists to forget the revivals of other styles and to act as if the line of derived Classical architecture in this country were as continuous from the beginning of the previous century as it was in France from the time of François I to that of Louis XIV.

As early as the seventies the admiration for Colonial architecture began. Although the earliest imitations are barely recognizable as such, by the time of Richardson's death the Colonial Revival was becoming the dominant influence in domestic design, as it has remained practically down to the present day. Also in the eighties, there began the imitation or, as it was called, the adaptation of Italian Renaissance design to modern uses. From this grew an academic public architecture comparable to that of the *Ecole des Beaux Arts* in France. This academic style was consecrated as official by the founding of the American Academy in Rome in the nineties. It was hailed generally as the "American Renaissance," as though the Renaissance, beginning in Italy in the fifteenth century, spreading to France in the sixteenth and seventeenth centuries and to England in the seventeenth and eighteenth had at last reached America at the end of the nineteenth. The first example of the new Italian adaptation, the Villard Houses in New York, by McKim, Mead & White (1883-85) and the first monumental and academic work of the same architects, the

RAYMOND HOOD: McGraw-Hill Building   New York, 1931

McKIM, MEAD & WHITE: Public Library   Boston, 1887-95

Boston Public Library (1887-95), were the finest the new movement was to produce.

When the "American Renaissance," nurtured in the East, was carried West to the Chicago World's Fair of 1893, the best of its possibilities had already been realized. But in the World's Fair there was imposed for the first time since the Greek Revival of the thirties a consistent program of classical design. The virtues of order in general planning, of consistency in scale and detail, of co-operation on a great project were very considerable. The World's Fair however, brought about the death of originality. The new attitude toward design accepted paper facades, derived from the European academic tradition, stretched over enormous edifices of metal skeleton construction. The integrity of Richardson's expression of masonry which was still present in McKim's Boston Public Library, and the boldness of Sullivan's expression of metal construction were disowned and soon forgotten in the buoyant glamour of a new Classical Revival.

At the same time the virtues of the Fair: order in group planning, consistency of design, the discipline of an accepted tradition and enthusiasm for thorough if limited training were impossible of continuance under American conditions. In Washington and elsewhere schemes for the "City Beautiful" attempted to make permanent the splendors of the Fair, only to fall afoul of unpredictable economic developments. The skyscrapers, although clothed in academic forms, fitted into no traditional scheme of urban design.

Architects, even the most gifted, found in the doctrine of adaptation not so much a discipline as an excuse for making use of all the new documentary riches of archæological detail which photography made increasingly available. Even the Gothic Revival, dying since the early seventies, had a new lease of life and was fastened again more firmly on churches and colleges without any of the vigorous although crude originality of the earlier day.

The only restraining criteria in all the new welter of revivalism and adaptation were *taste* and *correctness,* for the academic tradition had too short a root in this country to encourage the growth of positive canons of design. Too often the best buildings were the deadest. Those that showed some indications of

life appear as vulgar as the splendors of the age of Grant. An academic tradition might have been successfully founded and imposed with sufficient rigidity to give American cities some of the better qualities of the World's Fair of 1893. But the expanding assurance of the country was too great, the belief in individualism too strong, the pace of change too rapid to achieve the relative harmony and dignity which the nineteenth century gave to Paris, Vienna or London.

If one examines American architecture in bulk it is the productions of the last fifty years that one chiefly sees. The buildings of Richardson are few and hard to find; the early skyscrapers, even if they have not been destroyed, are lost beside the towering buildings which surround them. Prominent public buildings everywhere represent the most conspicuous results of academic revivalism; the more luxurious residence districts are like brief guide books to the styles of architecture; the business districts offer every conceivable stylistic device for covering skeleton metal construction with masonry design. Not all the individual edifices are without merit and even the worst often have a purely theatrical value as architectural entertainment. But nowhere does a coherent city picture exist. The integrated relationship which tied together the architectural treatment of various kinds of buildings and gave the early nineteenth century a consistency and a dignity is lacking today. Only factories and other industrial buildings—monuments of engineering, not of architecture—stand as honest representatives of modern

McKIM, MEAD & WHITE: The Villard Houses   New York, 1883-85

building amid the welter of paper surface design.

The new Classical buildings at Washington, the new Gothic or Georgian buildings at the leading universities, the skyscrapers, the movie theaters and churches in the cities, the palaces and the cottages in the suburbs—all built since the War—offer no new picture beyond that of the intentions of the nineties. All are splendid, expensive and meaningless. Worse, most of their architects have sacrificed convenience to splendor and swallowed up in display money which was needed for necessities. By perverting the meaning of all the stylistic features they have used, they have almost destroyed the hope of an original architecture. Dishonesty has often enough been financial as well as artistic. Bad design has too conspicuously been the expression of bad economics.

Behind the gaudy academic front with its utter lack of significant development there was nevertheless important work which continued the freer tradition of Richardson and Sullivan. Some houses in the East continued to be built in which, although the detail might be archæological, the massing and the planning were the direct outgrowth of American conditions and methods of wooden construction; some new types of construction, such as ferro-concrete (used after 1900 as frequently for low buildings as steel construction was for skyscrapers) failed to submit readily to adaptation; some critics, such as Montgomery Schuyler, did not forget entirely the achievements of Richardson and Sullivan in the nineteenth century.

Against this background of almost universally accepted revivalism Frank Lloyd Wright stands out, alone and original. His work and influence constitute a new chapter in modern architecture.

ALBERT KAHN: FORD PLANT   River Rouge, Michigan

CASS GILBERT: SUPREME COURT BUILDING   Washington, D. C., 1934

FRANK LLOYD WRIGHT: ROBIE HOUSE   Chicago, 1908-09

III. WRIGHT AND THE INTERNATIONAL STYLE
BY HENRY-RUSSELL HITCHCOCK, JR.

THERE WAS one prophet of modern architecture, relatively without honor in his own country but watched all over the world by those who hoped American architecture had not died with the nineteenth century. Frank Lloyd Wright has been far more isolated from the general current of his century than were Richardson and Sullivan in theirs. But his innovations have been more radical. If any one man may be considered the father of architecture in the second quarter of this century, it will probably be Wright.

He was a disciple of Sullivan; but where Sullivan's achievement was restricted to tall commercial structures, Wright has recreated all types of design. His earliest and most continuous success was with suburban dwelling houses, with which Richardson had done so much, and in which the tradition of free design continued most effectively. Even in his early houses, built just after the turn

of the century, Wright threw over all the traditions which Richardson himself had respected. His plans were not merely open; the living interior of the house was treated as a single complex space. His windows were not merely massed, as Richardson had massed them in his libraries; they formed bands the full length of the wall. Finally, his houses were not designed in terms of mass at all; they were conceived in terms of the skeleton; the walls became intersecting planes gathered beneath the covering planes of the wide-eaved, low-pitched roofs. He used various sorts of materials, although at the first rarely steel or concrete, and sought for them types of structural expression and even ornamental detail which were so logical as to appear wholly fresh and startling. Some of the most interesting of his houses were simple summer cottages, others were as large as the marble palaces of Eastern architects. Perhaps the finest is one of medium size, the Robie House in Chicago (1908) with its fine brickwork, its ship-like plan, and its splendid precision of execution.

At the same time, in his Larkin Administration Building in Buffalo (1904) and his Unity Temple in Oak Park (1905), he made parallel innovations in industrial and ecclesiastical architecture with brilliant experimental use of new materials.

In the years after 1910 he built less. The academic wave initiated at the Chicago Fair in 1893 had not at first submerged the West as completely as the East. Around Sullivan and Wright grew up a Chicago School of architects which accepted their leadership. But finally the West succumbed to academic revivalism and disowned Wright just when foreign publications were proclaiming him the only great architect in America.

In this decade Wright tended to become preoccupied with ornament as Sullivan had in his later years. In Wright's earlier work ornament had played but a small part. The Imperial Hotel in Tokio (1916), his largest building, although magnificent in plan and general conception is almost as meretriciously gaudy in its free way as the hotels of the academic architects in America in their revivalistic way.

In the twenties Wright found a new lease of life. Working in the Southwest he developed a different type of construction—precast concrete blocks with reinforcement in the joints—which encouraged a new and more rigid type of design. In the Millard House in Pasadena (1921) the blocks are all patterned. In the Jones House in Tulsa (1931) there are no patterns, and a new type of

FRANK LLOYD WRIGHT: ISABEL ROBERTS HOUSE   River Forest, Chicago, 1907

wall consisting of alternate vertical sections of concrete blocks and glass gives individual character to the design. Today Wright continues to experiment with new materials and to conduct near his home in Wisconsin a stimulating architectural school.

Wright, like Richardson, has had pupils, but they have rarely done more than imitate his manner for a few years without assimilating or developing it. Except for Irving Gill in California, who created out of a radical simplification of Spanish Colonial design a modern treatment of poured concrete construction for houses, Wright has been the only modern architect of consequence of the first quarter of the century in America.

Now, in the second quarter of this century, American architecture is much influenced by modern building in Europe since the War, which in turn found one of its chief inspirations in the early work of Wright. Open planning, composition in planes instead of in solid masses, horizontal lines, direct expression of construction, frank use of new materials, are the marks of what has been called the International Style of the present day. It is the International Style which has encouraged the return of Sullivan's horizontal style of skyscraper design. Indeed, Howe & Lescaze's Philadelphia Savings Fund Society Building is one of the most conspicuous monuments of the International Style to be found anywhere. For the most part, however, modernism in the skyscraper has meant little more than a substitution of block forms and non-traditional detail (usually copied from European work of the early twentieth century) for the academic embellishments and conventional forms of the skyscrapers of the past generation.

In the last few years international modern architecture has begun to influence fields of design other than the skyscraper. There are a few truly modern houses, none of them very distinguished; and although there has been little building, it is rather clear that the academic tradition is nearly at an end, while its major representatives retreat by compromising with the International Style, as Morris & O'Connor have done in the Avery Memorial in Hartford (1933).

New architectural problems such as the prefabricated house and inexpensive public housing hardly admit of traditional treatment. The chief model is the post-War work in European cities. Finally, the Century of Progress Exposition in Chicago in 1933 has sounded the death knell of archæological design, not because of the excellence of the modern work there (it was in part very bad indeed) but because all the build-

FRANK LLOYD WRIGHT: R. L. Jones House   Tulsa, Okla., 1931

HOWE & LESCAZE   Philadelphia, 1932
Philadelphia Saving Fund Society Building

LE CORBUSIER & PIERRE JEANNERIT: Savoye House   Poissy-sur-Seine, France, 1929-30

ings were in intention modern and were widely accepted by the same general public which forty years before was carried away by the academic splendors of the earlier World's Fair.

It is sad that there has been no development of a national modern architecture out of the work of Richardson or Sullivan or Wright. But at the opening of the middle third of the twentieth century it seems clear that the kind of free architecture which they in their separate ways achieved will now replace academic revivalism even though the new architecture has thus far drawn its inspiration chiefly from the work of Le Corbusier, Oud, Gropius and Mies van der Rohe in Europe. To the historians of the future, the multitudinous productions of the building boom in the twenties will doubtless seem as futile and fussy as those of the post-Civil War period. The present cessation of building has been difficult for American architects, but if it provides time for quiet assimilation and thoughtful development of the International Style it may be a boon for American architecture.

IV. THE MODERN ROOM
By Philip Johnson

MODERN INTERIOR architecture, decoration, and the design and arrangement of furniture are characterized by simplicity and governed by utility. The impression created by the modern room should be one of space and lightness. Instead of an accumulation of objects the room should present a homogeneous

and harmonious background for modern living.

These principles of simplicity and functionalism create an effect very different from the peculiar and fantastic style aberration known as "modernistic." It is unfortunate that the word "modern" as applied to buildings, furniture and

decoration should have become so identified in the public mind with "modernistic." This confusion of terms must be cleared up if people are ever to overcome their hesitancy in accepting the modern style. They are justified in refusing to admit into their homes anything modernistic.

Styles in interior decoration follow one another like styles in women's clothes. The "modernistic" with its zigzags, setbacks and tortured angles merely redesigns the surfaces of furniture and rooms. The same cornices and moldings, the same sideboards and mantels are given a new surface treatment. A modernistic chair, for example, is simply an old-style chair attempting to look modern. Its curves are replaced by freakish angles; geometric or cubistic designs are used in its upholstery patterns. In principle, however, it is nothing but the same old chair carrying a new burden of ornament.

The functional modern approach, on the other hand, goes beneath the surface to fundamentals. The word "modern" means nothing more than up-to-date, but in its application to house building, decoration and furnishing it means up-to-date in a very thorough and complete sense. First, it involves taking into consideration the tremendous changes in the mechanics of living that the past twenty

HOWE & LESCAZE: Field House   New Hartford, Conn., 1933

or even ten years have brought about. Second, it takes the utmost advantage of the technical achievements of our age. Third, it uses the new materials and the new methods of construction that have been developed in recent years. And first, last, and always, it dares question traditional forms and discard them if they have outlived their functions. On the other hand, it never makes a surface change merely for the sake of producing something "different." A modern chair is quite different in appearance from a traditional chair, but every change in it is predicated upon reason. Modern technics have evolved the steel tube. Used as the frame of a chair, its strength makes unnecessary a great deal of the bulk needed for a wooden frame. The fact that steel is flexible makes box springs unnecessary. There is no make-believe or useless complication in really modern furniture. Not only in furniture, but in building and decoration the two cardinal principles of modern style are utility and simplicity.

In traditional rooms it has long been the custom to ignore the specific and multiple uses to which a room will be put. Instead, the room is given a name —living room, dining room, bedroom, etc.—and is furnished according to custom rather than reason. In designing a modern living room the interior architect considers specifically what activities will take place in the room when occupied by one, two or a number of persons. All the furniture for the room is then selected definitely with these individual or combined activities in mind. The functional placement of the furniture, where it may best serve these purposes, is the next consideration. Thus, instead of placing a desk where it would symmetrically fill a wall composition, it is placed apart from the general group of chairs and in a position where the light would be best for writing. Also the chairs, instead of being placed formally far from each other—each with its little table for ashtrays and glasses—may be grouped facing a low central table.

As the modern room is a background for living, it must be both simple in appearance and efficient in service. Simplicity is achieved by the elimination of superfluous objects and all purely ornamental features. Efficiency is attained by the use of materials and designs that best serve the purposes for which they are intended, whether or not they have ever before been put to such use. Simplicity and utility combined produce a very satisfying kind of beauty. A heavy piece of glass, for example, is the best possible top for a tea table. It is easily cleaned and is ornamental. Chromium steel legs supporting the glass top are efficient, for

APARTMENT J, NEW YORK—Furniture by Miës van der Rohe

JAN RUHTENBERG: Apartment Living Room, 1930

RICHARD J. NEUTRA: LOVELL HOUSE   Los Angeles, 1929

steel gives the greatest amount of strength per unit of material. This combination of polished steel and crystal-clear glass results in a beautiful and unusual tea table. By using the most efficient materials, many details of construction heretofore considered necessary may be eliminated. Furniture becomes lighter in appearance and in that way contributes to the feeling of space in the room. For the prettiness of carved detail and patterned materials, modern decoration substitutes the beauty of un-

broken surfaces of grained wood and the natural texture-patterns and weave of raw silk, wool and other fabrics.

Probably the most striking and essential change from the traditional treatment of a room, however, results from the wholly different approach of the modern designer. The old-style interior decorator regards the room as a box to enclose people and things and therefore to be ornamented inside. The modern interior architect considers the room a series of interrelated planes to be ar-

ranged for maximum beauty and utility. He rejects the thought of an enclosure of walls, ceiling and floor that crowd in upon one. To get away from the conception of a room as a tight box, with the floor joined firmly to the walls and the walls to the ceiling, he treats these surfaces as separate, unbroken planes extending indefinitely — cut but not stopped by one another. Instead of giving each window its own curtain, he covers the entire window wall with a curtain that extends from ceiling to floor and from side to side, making a plane of cloth that intersects the side walls. The floor has a single covering of carpet or linoleum, unpatterned. This allows the floor to sink away from one's consciousness instead of rising to demand one's attention with a welter of rugs and vari-colored patterns. The neutral-toned, single floor covering seems also to enlarge the room. In everything done to the room an effort is made to increase the impression of space and freedom. Cornices are omitted, and window and door trims reduced to a minimum in order to break as little as possible the simple planes of the walls.

The simplicity of the modern room is a perfect setting to enhance the beauty of natural things and of genuine works of art. In it bright-colored bookbindings, flowers and plants and, above all, paintings and sculpture are far more effective. In fact, even people in the room seem more colorful and alive. The idea of the room as a decorator's box to be prettified is passing. The modern room fulfills its purpose only as a background for modern living.

V. THE MODERN HOUSE
By Philip Johnson

MAN'S FIRST house was a cave—a place of shelter from the elements and of protection from his enemies. Shelter and protection—or privacy—are still the primary functions of a man's house, with comfort added as the third essential.

To the primary housing needs civilization and progress have added a host of lesser requirements, and houses have evolved accordingly. Within the past few decades, however, structural advances have been so remarkable and revolutionary that our entire concept of house-building must change not only to keep pace with the times but to reap the advantages made available by modern invention and improvement. The type of building today that has made greatest use of new methods and materials is the modern factory with its flat roof, glass walls and steel post construction.

There are two reasons why a man

RICHARD J. NEUTRA: ANNA STEN HOUSE   Los Angeles, 1934

building a house for his home shies away from the construction efficiency used in building factories. In the first place, "efficiency" as applied to house-building has an ugly sound to him. It threatens to destroy the beauty and sentiment of his home. In the second place, he is so accustomed to traditional house patterns that he cannot readily visualize any dwelling that does not conform to one or another of the patterns—Georgian, Colonial, California-Spanish or variations and combinations of them. Whether or not he distinguishes them by name, he is so used to them that he believes anything radically different would look "funny."

For this reason, houses are still being built almost always from the outside in. That is, the exterior style is decided upon and the interior arrangement must conform to it. For example, it is no longer necessary for the outer walls to support a house and hold up the roof; post construction supplies the support and instead of small windows perforating thick, opaque walls, an entire wall may be made of glass. But that would indeed make a house of any traditional style look "funny." Therefore, in building a modern house, it is necessary to rid ourselves of all preconceived ideas on the subject.

The modern house is built from the inside out. No exterior pattern is decided upon; the outward shape and appearance is determined by the inner arrangement of the rooms and, most of all, by the needs and desires of the occupants of the house. A modern house on a city lot might be built somewhat in the following fashion, the entire lot or ground space being considered integrally with the house. First comes the placement of the house—its position decided solely on the basis of adding to the pleasure and comfort of its occupants. A city street is apt to be noisy and dirty; therefore the service rooms—kitchen, laundry, etc.—are placed on the street side. The garage is placed there also and is no longer a separate building but part of the house. This consolidation of house and garage is far more convenient and more economical, as one foundation, one roof, and one heating system serves both. Furthermore, it releases extra ground space in the back for the garden. And to make the garden as large as possible, the house is placed as near the street as the building law allows.

The living section of the house is on the garden side. In fact, the garden is practically an extension of the living room, for only a glass wall separates the two and in pleasant weather there is no separation, as the glass wall opens

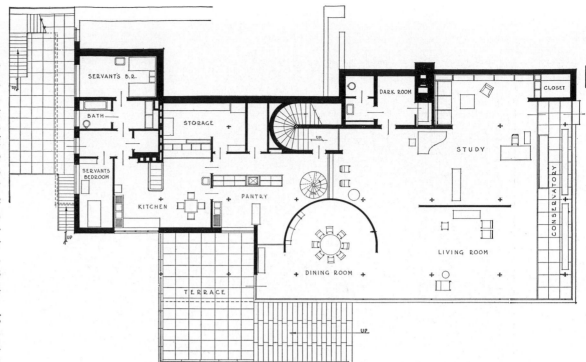

MIËS VAN DER ROHE: TUGENDHAT HOUSE   Brno, Czechoslovakia, 1930

wide. Because modern construction methods make a low-sunk foundation weather-tight and water-tight, the floor of the living room is practically on a level with the garden and furniture may easily be shifted from one to the other.

The interior arrangement of the rooms on the lower floor is as open as possible. These are the rooms that a family uses in common; there is little need for privacy here. Therefore the rooms flow into one another, their separateness being indicated by spur or partial walls. Yet each shares the light, ventilation and spaciousness of all. The floor above is supported by slender posts. The advantages of this method of open planning are shown in the plan above. The plan also shows the modern type of conservatory, which is formed by a double glass wall along one side of the living room. The plants are grown in the long,

narrow space between the two walls—a modernly efficient arrangement superior to the old-fashioned conservatory. It is especially practical in houses that must be built in space limited by a crowding city.

On the second floor the bedrooms are built with the ordinary separation walls, but the windows run in a solid horizontal band. In accordance with the cardinal principles of modern architecture—simplicity and usefulness—each bedroom may be designed to serve not only as a sleeping chamber but as a private living room or study as well. The bed is the only piece of furniture in the room that conspicuously belongs in a bedroom and nowhere else. But if it is placed properly in relation to the other pieces of furniture in the room, it may be closed off from them during the day by a curtain that can be opened wide at night.

HOWE & LESCAZE: FIELD HOUSE   New Hartford, Conn., 1933

HOWARD T. FISHER: Logan House   Northbrook, Ill., 1934

KOCHER & FREY: Week End House   Near Northport, Long Island, 1934

HOWE & LESCAZE   New York, 1934
Lescaze House

By hanging the curtain from ceiling to floor and from side to side, it will be in effect a wall and the remainder of the space will form a private living room or study.

Another efficient feature of the modern bedroom is the elimination of closets and chests of drawers. Instead of these, cabinets are built in along one entire side of the room, the sliding doors that conceal them composing a paneled wall.

The outward appearance of the modern house conforms to the interior arrangement of rooms. With this arrangement to work with the architect then harmonizes the windows, doors and other exterior elements in a balance and rhythm. The result is usually asymmetrical because of the informal interior arrangement. The long window bands make a primarily horizontal design broken by the occasional verticals of a chimney or a stairwell. In place of traditional symmetrical ordering of facades the rhythm is one of even regularity following the regularity of the construction skeleton. The beauty of a modern facade is the beauty of balanced rectangles, window areas and wall areas, rather than the attractiveness of ornamented window and door treatment, or the picturesqueness of a gable roof and dormer window.

VI. HOUSE AND CITIES

By Catherine Bauer

MOST OF us have some sort of shelter with four walls, a roof and a floor, to which we repair when we need rest, privacy, refreshment or the company of family and friends. For most of us this dwelling is closely surrounded by a great many other dwellings, by stores, factories, offices, schools, movie-palaces, railroad stations and a hundred other kinds of building—all of them tied together by a complicated network of pavement, pipes, wires and tracks. Both houses and cities, then, are part of our daily experience.

On the other hand, "housing" and "city planning" have meant for most of us only the remotest sort of abstraction. If we have used the terms at all, it was only in connection with some special undertaking — philanthropic rehabilitation of an ancient slum district, for instance, or putting through a handsome and showy boulevard. "Housing" had nothing to do with our own houses. "City planning" was strictly limited to certain superficial aspects of city development.

The ordinary methods of constructing average human environment seemed to present no special problem. Any family of normal ambition could, it was assumed, buy a nice piece of land and erect thereon a decent home, becoming thus both respectable and secure. Houses in the future would doubtless have more and better bathrooms, newer and trickier gadgets. Skyscrapers would be taller and have faster elevators; subways would be longer and quicker; land-values higher and wider. The problem of traffic congestion would somehow be solved by double-decker streets or vertical parking elevators, or perhaps by cheap airplanes.

Seldom indeed, as the houses multiplied to infinity and the cities swallowed up the countryside for miles around, did we look at these things objectively, or evaluate them in terms of real human convenience and amenity. We did not stop to question the strange fact that houses had doubled in cost while automobiles had been halved and quartered in price. If we were sometimes vaguely dissatisfied with the lack of sun or air or outlook in our home, or its distance from our work and play places, we accepted these drawbacks philosophically and hoped to get an electric refrigerator instead. High taxes we attributed, grumbling, to "corruption." Never did we have any fundamental doubts as to the premises and practices underlying our methods of producing human environment.

But suddenly today our indifference has been changed to a sense of urgent necessity. What happened in the realm of abstract economics is reflected even more dramatically, if that be possible, in the physical world of houses and cities. Something is vitally wrong, and something drastic must be done about it. "Housing" and "city planning" have become great issues which affect the life and living of every citizen.

Before we consider what should be done we must acquaint ourselves with what was done in the past. American cities have historic periods quite as clearly defined and as significant as the Romanesque-Gothic-Baroque of European towns. Let us see what these periods are and what heritage they have left us. Every layer of man-made environment crystallizes a whole set of purposes and beliefs. What forces shaped the building of Chicago and Pittsburgh, of Topeka and Tallahassee?

THE FRONTIER SETTLEMENT: EVERY MAN FOR HIMSELF

The majority of American towns were settled by individuals who had left the old centers of civilization, either on the Eastern seaboard or in Europe, in order to "seek their fortunes." Only rarely were these settlers unified by any collective purpose or common background. Virtues they had aplenty, but they were the individualistic virtues of the pioneer: initiative, personal courage and ambition, self-sufficiency, ingenuity, hardihood. As soon as a man grew restless or dissatisfied with his neighbors or his situation, he "moved on" into the wilderness where there was more elbow-room.

But the virtues of the pioneer are not, by and large, the virtues which produce handsome, efficient, permanent centers of civilization. Such cities are necessarily the result of harmonious communal enterprise and group responsibility. Individuals must work with other individuals for a common end, subordinating thereto certain personal interests and ambitions. Whatever the political-economic framework may be, architecture is essentially a collective art. Many mid-Western cities still have that air of impermanence, as if the citizens were just preparing to move on, that characterized all of them when first they were being worked for their gold or oil or iron. But perhaps our deepest heritage from the frontier was the ideal of "individual" houses, designed, built and owned by the resident, and surrounded on all four sides by as large a piece of land as possible. A man's house was his fortress, his defense against all the other members of a predatory society, symbol of his success and expression of his personality. So strong is this ideal still, even in the midst of congested apartments and mass-produced bungalows, that few Americans can realize how different it is from the ideal which produced the great city civilizations of Europe. Nor do they realize how impossible of achievement it is within the complex network of modern urban society. The pioneer who felt crowded when there was another hut within two miles of him is reflected today in the miles of deep, narrow, "individual" frame houses which dot the suburbs of any American town.

Moreover, the habit of "mine and move," of competitive exploitation for quick profits, was not confined to mineral wealth. From the beginning, the same practice was applied to that primary resource of the city, land itself.

BOOSTER PLANNING: PROGRESS BY ARITHMETIC

Almost all American cities were "planned," in a very real sense. Not only were streets and lots laid out in advance of use, but they were laid out with a definite purpose in mind. That purpose had little or nothing to do with ultimate convenience, efficiency or beauty, and was modified only with great difficulty to allow for a minimum of sanitation and safety. The accepted end of all "development," the conscious or unconscious purpose of all "planning," was a maximum of quick profit for the developer. The mechanical gridiron plan, with its hills leveled off and its valleys filled in, with its standardized blocks and lots and its undifferentiated streets without beginning or end, was the ideal pattern for this purpose. It provided a maximum of "front feet," easily negotiable because they were "standard" and highly speculative because no one could possibly predict the ultimate future use.

New York City itself is one of the prime examples of this profit-planning. As early as 1807 the ambitious city fathers made a gridiron city-plan covering the whole of Manhattan (the existing town was then only a small village down around the Battery) with absolutely standardized streets and lots, regardless of topography, possible future use, or any other non-statistical consideration. The whole island became one vast parcel of speculative commodities.

The same mechanical measures and purely quantitative standards carried

Outright Slums, Pennsylvania mining town

"Own Your Own Home" slums, Long Island

Blight, Chaos and Dilapidation, Chicago

Row housing with yards blocked by garages and alleys, Long Island

Megalopolitan Congestion, New York

New Law tenements, Manhattan

HERITAGE OF THE LAST CENTURY   TWENTIETH CENTURY HOUSING IN AMERICA

over into other matters. The prosperity of cities was gauged entirely by such matters as the rate of population-growth, the increase in lot prices, the mileage of paved streets and utility lines, average wealth per capita regardless of its distribution, the number of new industrial plants and stores, etc. All of these matters were thought of as statistical curves of progress, produceable to infinity.

With the appearance of enormous centralized junction-towns, in which all numerical records were broken, congestion itself became a symbol of prosperity. Small towns which had once been spacious did their best to ape the unwieldy chaos of Metropolis, skyscrapers, tenements and all. There was no sense of the city as an organism which, if it is to to function efficiently, has certain inherent limitations on form and growth.

City governments themselves encouraged and speculated on their own indefinite spread. Endless paved streets and utility lines were laid out long in advance of any possible use, to facilitate lot speculation. By 1929 almost every progressive city had enough lots staked out to take care of several times its actual population. Those miles of unused concrete and rotting pipes are today among the most dramatic monuments to the New Era and one of the prime causes of municipal bankruptcy.

THE HOUSES: FROM DIM IDEAL TO DIFFERENT REALITY

The houses which were built in such enormous numbers in the spreading suburbs were not, perforce, designed with much attention to real human needs or real technical or material possibilities. They had to be fitted into the rigid limitations of a completely mechanical scheme in whatever manner would bring the largest immediate profit to the builder. Land and utilities were increasingly expensive; every bit of open space was just so much "waste."

Land speculation (gambling, that is, on the possibilities of future congestion) was a potent factor in determining the actual form of the American home, as distinct from that vague frontier ideal of secluded individual mansions. In addition, there was a growing body of complicated "building restrictions," the result of sheer vital necessity, which legalized the congestion and pegged up both construction and land costs, but which did at the same time attempt to enforce certain crude minima of safety and sanitation.

Together, these two forces shaped the average homes of the past fifty years: "one-family houses" four to eight feet apart; bungalows; "duplexes"; three-

and four-decker flats; tenements covering three quarters of the site or more. The majority of them were mass-produced by small speculative builders. What a far cry they were from that magazine-cover "ideal home" which was still being promoted as a real possibility!

THE CITY BEAUTIFUL: ORNAMENTAL PATCHWORK

From about the beginning of the century onward, there were signs of reaction against the barrack-towns of the nineteenth century. But this reaction did not, unfortunately, carry with it enough vitality of purpose or understanding to put through any fundamental changes.

The Great White City of the Chicago World's Fair of 1893, together with Burnham's plan for Chicago, galvanized a fairly wide-spread interest in the tags of Renaissance city-planning—an interest which had been more or less moribund in America since L'Enfant planned Washington. Avenues and parkways, vistas and perspectives, radicals and rond-points, duly punctuated with large white public buildings as nearly "classic" as possible, became the objective of all civic-minded individuals. "Civic centers" were planned, and some of them were executed. But, outside of a certain amount of admirable park-planning, perhaps the best inheritance of many American cities, most of these earnest efforts amounted to little more than surface show.

At the same time the new yearning for "culture" (which invariably signified past European culture) had an even more obvious effect on residential exteriors. The experiments of the seventies and eighties, often crude and vulgar but lively and imaginative nevertheless, gave way to a period of worried "good taste" which has lasted up to the present. All the literature on past "styles" was ransacked, and the houses of the rich were faithful copies of Tudor, Italian, Norman or "Colonial" villas. Middle-class houses were vulgarized copies of the houses of the rich. (The houses of the poor were, of course, the cast-offs of another generation and were not supposed to be tasteful.)

The net effect of the whole movement was merely, all in all, to reinforce and bedizen the earlier pattern, which underneath remained quite as chaotic and exploitive as ever. No matter what monumental effect was contrived for the center, the city continued to spread out at the edge in a rash of amorphous subdivisions over which the city-planners had no control whatsoever, and indeed, asked none. And, no matter how letter-perfect they might be individually, a

street full of French, Italian and Olde Englishe houses, each competing with the other for the attention and approbation of the passer-by, is an architectural monstrosity. A congested tenement, whether it is on Chrystie Street or Park Avenue and whether it has a Gothic or baroque vestibule or merely a dingy "hall," is still nothing more nor less than a congested tenement.

OLD METHODS HAVE BROKEN DOWN

Now that the fever of expansion has subsided, we are beginning to discover that most of the houses built twenty years ago are already downright slums, and that a large proportion of those put up since the war are well on the way toward "blight" and decay. That great traditional symbol of security, home-ownership, has become an empty mockery in the face of wholesale foreclosure, of houses not worth half the amount of the mortgage, of dwellings which are slums ten years after construction. Brand new skyscrapers are half empty—white elephants whose owners would gladly give them away if they could.

Cities which predicated a smoothly rising population-curve, and gauged their finances accordingly, are losing thousands of their former citizens without gaining any new ones. Taxes levied on future speculative "values" are not being paid, and municipalities burdened with expensive subways and miles of unused streets and sewers are being forced to cut down on schools and hospitals and libraries. The most prosperous, fastest-growing towns of the twenties are today the most hopelessly bankrupt.

The end of the downward curve is not yet in sight. For the situation is no mere phenomenon of temporary depression: it is a sign that a whole era has run its course. The old hit-or-miss, speculative, individualist methods had, even before 1929, failed to provide new dwellings of any standard of decency for any but the richest third of the population. At present they have broken down completely and produce no dwellings at all. The American nineteenth century environment, based on a belief in uncontrolled speculative enterprise and on a sentiment for pioneering individualism, is an obsolete pattern. What shall we put in its place?

PLANNING FOR PROFIT—OR FOR USE?

If we are to build houses and cities adequate to the needs of the twentieth century, we must start all over again,

Pittsburgh

The Bronx, N. Y.

Rotterdam, Holland

Frankfurt, Germany

BACKYARDS: TWO CONTRASTS IN PLANNING

from the ground up. Many of our preconceived notions as to what a house or a city should look like must be altered. We must build from a fresh set of premises. We must be prepared to scrap much of the physical, sentimental and financial heritage of the past fifty years. And finally, we must be ready to fight those forces whose vested interest in the old scheme of things makes them bitter enemies of change.

What are houses and cities made of? Physically speaking—land, labor and materials. We have an ample supply of land. We have thousands of highly skilled building workers, most of them at present entirely without employment. Tons of materials are rotting in warehouses or being artificially kept from production. New improved processes and techniques are available but are not being used.

What are houses and cities made for? Their only real purpose, when all is said and done, ought to be human protection, convenience, comfort, health and pleasure. They must provide opportunity for privacy, and also for social intercourse. They must offer labor-saving devices, without making us slaves of machinery. They must be so arranged that all kinds of work and play can be carried on with a minimum of wasteful friction. They must be satisfactory to

the eye and the other senses, both in details and in the whole.

Architects and technicians and planners have in recent years been devising methods and techniques for building just such a human environment. Much scientific knowledge, hitherto unusued, can at last be put to human service. Why should not these rich resources, this new knowledge, be used to replace our obsolete equipment with houses and cities designed to meet efficiently the most complex human requirements?

Why not indeed? These premises seem very simple and obvious. And yet, outside of a few difficult experiments, they never entered into the production of nineteenth century environment or into the houses and cities which we live in today.

The path is not entirely uncharted. In Europe much has already been achieved—several million modern dwellings built in planned communities by non-profit, non-competitive enterprise, and let at rents within reach of average citizens. Housing has become a "public utility," and the unit of plan, of design, of construction and of administration is the complete neighborhood, equipped from the start with all the facilities for a well-rounded social life and for productive leisure. In America there have been a few such experiments,

and some of the government projects now under construction will provide a few more.

Out of the European experience has grown already a new kind of architecture. It has been called "functionalism," which means merely that sun and air and human convenience and modern techniques become integral elements in architectural design. Forms are devised which can directly employ the most efficient modern materials and methods. Empty, pretentious, "styled" façades are eliminated and a truly modern architecture becomes possible. Instead of the monotonous repetition of jerry-built Tudor villas, standard parts are used to build up harmonious groups. Architecture, after more than two hundred years as an expression of snobbishness and "conspicuous waste," comes into its own once more as the mother of the arts and a fitting expression for a working social organism.

Can we have good houses, efficient cities and modern architecture in America? There are two major conditions. We must be willing to plan for *use* and not for profit. And above all, as consumers, as workers, as individuals, as families, as citizens, as voters, we must want a better living environment enough to fight for it.

IV. Stage Design

By JOHN MASON BROWN

PLAYGOERS IN the contemporary theater are asked to do very little work. For the most part we can check our imaginations with our hats. We do not have to clothe our dramas in settings of our own imagination, as the Elizabethans did. Dramatists today rely upon the collaboration of scenic artists. They do not need to exhort us, as Shakespeare did the groundlings of Elizabeth's day, to "piece out our imperfections with your thoughts." We take it as a matter of course that when the curtain is raised we shall see a stage meticulously set to meet the needs of the particular play which is to be acted. And it is made very easy for us to pretend that the curtain is a fourth wall removed from the room inhabited by those characters whose fortunes we are asked to follow for a brief two hours.

We are thoroughly aware that the room we look into, as through a giant keyhole, is not an actual room, and that the forest in which this or that scene occurs is not an actual forest. But this does not disturb us; in fact, we accept this convention of the theater quite automatically. For as Coleridge pointed out, the fundamental premise upon which the theater depends for the illusion it creates, is a "suspension of disbelief" on the part of the audience.

Among those who today make it very easy for us to accept the illusion of the theater are the stage designers, whose job it is to realize the intentions of our dramatists in visual terms. Present-day designers belong to a comparatively recent development of theater art. They are products of a movement—known defiantly enough as "The New Movement in the Theater"—which, due to the inspiration of such leaders as Gordon Craig and Adolphe Appia and the Russian painters who turned to the stage at the end of the last century, has changed the course and emphasis of the modern theater.

When the Hallams, a company of English actors, first came to this country in the middle of the eighteenth century, most theaters relied upon six regulation changes of scenery which were the standbys of their repertories. These changes, which were so essential to the operation of all American playhouses, were mothered by the production needs of the time. Historically they were derived from the three types of setting invented in the sixteenth century by the Italian, Sebastiano Serlio, and were similar to the changes of scenery used by the French dramatist, Molière. They consisted of a wood, a street, a parlor, a kitchen and a palace. There were three wings or side scenes at each side, and borders above. As the nineteenth century went its way settings became heavier and heavier and increasingly realistic. Of this realistic tendency Belasco was the great exponent in America. His duplication of a Childs restaurant led Arthur Hopkins to complain that the only remarkable thing about such settings was that they were *not* real.

Modern theater design has come a long way from the days of hack scene-painters who used to set our stages with wood-wings and backdrops painted in false perspective. It is happily different in purpose and execution from the work of those daubers who in the smaller vaudeville houses and older stock companies used to spend their lives painting thyroidal leaves on fish-net borders and

JONES
SETTING FOR *Mourning Becomes Electra*

Photo Vandamm

GEDDES
SETTING FOR *The Divine Comedy*

tion of scenic artists, headed by Jo Miel-ziner and Donald Oenslager, to whom a third generation is even now about to be added, with Albert Johnston as its already established leader. The New Movement is, in other words, old and the points for which it battled are now as dead as only victorious causes in art can be. But because of these men and women, and the high gifts they have brought the theater, our contemporary stage is a far more stimulating and satis-fying place than it would ever have been if they had not believed in themselves as artists, and if as artists they had not suc-ceeded in having their say behind the footlights.

Examples of the work of these design-ers show how vital a part they play on our modern stage. Robert Edmond Jones' setting for *Mourning Becomes Electra* suggests, in terms which are glowingly theatrical, the parallel be-tween the New England house of the Mannons and the palace of Agamemnon. In his project for the theatrical presen-tation of Dante's *Divine Comedy*, Nor-man-Bel Geddes has, with the fervor of a poet, translated a poet's dream into visual terms. In Lee Simonson's rail-road bridge in *Liliom* realism is seen at its selective best. In Jo Mielziner's set for *Yellow Jack* the production of a many-scened chronicle play about sci-ence is not only made possible but heightened by the varying levels of a "sculptural stage." In Donald Oenslag-er's backgrounds for *The Emperor Jones* the trees increasingly take on the primi-

drop curtains of the Grand Canal on which advertisements for chewing gum, scalp lotion and baby powders rudely challenged the temporal sway of the Doges. Theater designers today are artists who must be judged by the power of imagination and selection which they show as interpreters working in a chal-lenging medium. They realize the fal-lacy of the older two-dimensional settings which the Hallams were accus-tomed to employ, which such a charm-ing dilletante as Major André used to amuse himself by painting, and which were standbys even in the nineteenth century theater. They know that these backdrops took everything into consid-eration except the three-dimensional bodies of the actors who played in front of them, and that these actors seemed to grow larger instead of smaller as they walked away from the audience and approached those lines which converged on the backdrops at the scene-painter's whim. They do not esteem the over-documented and cluttered settings by means of which David Belasco sought to reproduce reality behind his foot-lights. They have turned their backs on mere photography.

Since the first years of the World War, contemporary American stage designers —men such as Robert Edmond Jones, Lee Simonson, Norman-Bel Geddes— have brought a new beauty and a new

technical standard into our theater. To the ranks of these designers, and to such of their contemporaries as Aline Bern-stein, Livingston Platt, Raymond Sovey, Cleon Throckmorton and Woodman Thompson, has come a second genera-

SIMONSON
SETTING FOR *Liliom*

Photo by Bruguière

tive Congo forms that take possession of the mind of O'Neill's hero.

These examples do not, however, make clear special problems which the stage designer must face in the execution of his work. A scenic artist cannot simply make a sketch—a charming sketch of a room, for instance, with flowing stairs, high windows, a great door at the back, and figures posed in vague but graceful attitudes—and consider his job done. His job is much more extensive and more difficult than his sketches on the walls of an exhibition room may indicate.

Although, like the painter, he achieves his compositions within a frame, that is, within the proscenium arch, the stage designer cannot create an arbitrary and unchanging arrangement as the painter can. The painter builds up his composition, confident that it will remain fixed, stationary, as he paints it. His problems of arrangement do not include that of movement, the actual movement of figures against the background he designs. The stage designer, on the other hand, must think and compose in terms of movement. He must not only accommodate his backgrounds to the shifting positions of single actors, but make them equally hospitable to large crowds. He works in terms not of one grouping but of many groupings. His setting must house not one action but many actions, and serve the full flux of the unfolding drama. His composition is also subject to changing effects of light and color. He cannot depend, as the painter can, upon one unchanging source of light or the fixed values that certain colors possess. The designer's first thought must be whether or not his scheme has theatrical as well as compositional values. Does it meet the requirements of the text? Does it have the asset of display, which can transform a mere coming on to the stage into an entrance? And will his colors, which seem so pleasant in his sketch, maintain their values when they are subjected to the changes lighting will effect?

But the designer's work is not completed with the making of the design. The stage designer's drawing is, as Lee Simonson once observed, only "a record

OENSLAGER
SETTING FOR *The Emperor Jones*

of intention." It gives no indication of the actual work he must do. For when he has settled on his ground plan, had it approved by the director, the manager-producer, the carpenter, and often by the leading actor, made blueprints for every scene in elaborate detail, and tracked down the proper furniture and accessories, the scenic artist still has plenty of work ahead of him. He must get bids from the studios at which his scenery is to be painted; superintend the painting; see that the carpenters are not making his columns square when they should be round; make certain that everything will be done on time; make arrangements to have his scenery carted to the right theater; look after its hanging, its lighting; and be ready to make those last minute shifts and readjustments which, for one reason or another, always seem to be necessary in the theater.

If our best contemporary designers are too often asked to act as third-rate interior decorators, rather than as scenic artists, if they must turn out endless kitchens-in-the-Bronx when their minds are filled with dreams of the castle of Elsinore, they are not to be blamed. Their first duty is to the dramatists, and their talents are bound by the limitations of the plays they serve. Although they are too often forced to waste their energies upon literalistic scripts devoid of all inspiration, still it must be admitted that stage designers add much to the theater. More than we are apt to realize, they manage to lend color and excitement and beauty to the make-believe upon which the theater depends for its success.

With Shaw's Louis Dubedat, the American stage designer of today believes in the "might of design, the mystery of color, and the redemption of all things by beauty everlasting." He believes in the truth of Victor Hugo's words: "The place where this or that catastrophe occurs becomes a terrible and inseparable witness thereof; and the absence of silent characters of this sort would make the greatest scenes of history incomplete in the drama." The stage designer's aim is to make the setting an "inseparable witness" of the scene, a "silent character" without which the drama would be incomplete.

MATTHEW B. BRADY
WARD IN ARMORY SQUARE HOSPITAL, WASHINGTON, D. C.

V. Photography in the United States

By LINCOLN KIRSTEIN

THE HISTORY of the camera and of its uses in America is, in its comparatively restricted field, as interesting as it is complex. Because of its esthetic overtones photography demands the definitions due a fine art. Yet its inclusion among the fine arts is tempered considerably by its scientific origin and method. In fact, any discussion of photography inevitably involves these questions: Is it a scientific method or an artistically creative medium? Are photographs simply scientific and historical documents, or are they in their own right works of art? Do they stand comparison with the products of paintbrush and chisel, as they must if they are to be considered works of art?

To understand this basic split between art and science in photography one must explore the ancestry of the camera. The invention of modern photographic apparatus was the result of a series of discoveries in chemistry and optics. Aristotle observed the phenomenon of photosynthesis in green plants, a change in chemical constitution brought about by the action of light. Sixteenth century alchemists, searching for a means to change base metal to gold, discovered that certain silver compounds are sensi-

tive to light. The "camera obscura," a simple and ancient device consisting of a black box with a prism fixed to admit light, clearly reflecting the image outside, was employed by painters in the eighteenth century as an aid in perspective and scene painting. The two lines of development, chemical and optical, fused in 1802 when the potter, Wedgwood, trying to find a short cut for taking silhouettes, made shadow pictures on a silver nitrate base. The image always faded, however, until in 1839 Herschel suggested to the French scene painter, Daguerre, the use of sodium thiosulphate as a fixative. By the use of this "hypo," now familiar to every photographer, the permanence of the photographic image was technically assured. Daguerre's invention soon reached New York, and a Professor Draper of New York University succeeded in the experiment of photographing his daughter, who had to pose, steadily rigid, for ten minutes.

At first photography was considered simply a scientific aid to painters and artisans, but as it developed under progressive chemical research it began to assume the importance of an independent craft. Thus, soon after its incep-

tion, a change in its nature and in its function took place. Photography as an independent craft obviously trespassed upon the territory of other pictorial arts, and this fact brought about some confusion as to the esthetics of photography —a confusion which has continued to our own day.

The esthetics of an art or even of a very simple craft cannot be easily set forth. Photography, however, has certain inherent limitations which restrict its possibilities, and these limitations become evident in the definition of its rather simple technique. Photography is a clipping of the continuum of time and sight: the preservation of an instantaneous image. The image appears on a flat surface, recording on this single plane an identical and objective impression of what the eye sees. Principles of formal composition and subject selection apply in photography as well as in painting, though in a less marked degree, and the photographic medium is rich in possibilities of tonal quality and suggestive light. Except when consciously avoided, there is a large angle of accident in the taking of a picture, and this accidental quality, with all its elements of surprise and sudden arrest, contrib-

MATTHEW B. BRADY
HANOVER JUNCTION STATION

ALICE BOUGHTON
BY THE BROOK (Soft-focus photography)

utes not a little to the special nature of photography. The element of accident does not, of course, enter in the same degree into the arts of painting and sculpture.

From the beginning conflicting opinions about the function of photography were evident. Painters whose aim was the exact reproduction of nature were alarmed by the greater accuracy and facility of the new invention. They feared solemnly for the future of painting. But the camera was welcomed by others as a new and fascinating medium.

A man who belonged to the latter category was Matthew B. Brady, America's first great photographer. He had been sent to Paris to study painting in the company of that other artist-scientist, Samuel F. B. Morse. Like Degas and other French artists, he had admired the "metallic beauty" of Daguerre's

pictures, and on his return to New York he opened one of the increasingly popular "Daguerrian Parlors." The early portraits of Brady, notably those of the freaks in P. T. Barnum's museum, have a sincerity, clarity and honest brilliance not found in the work of his contemporaries. A great subject may often accelerate the development of a good craftsman, and it was Brady's luck to pass through the American Civil War. Of this impressive conflict, in all save its most violently active aspects where he was limited by the failure of time exposure, Brady has left an equally impressive record. In the blue volumes of the *Photographic History of the Civil War* we can see, as in a mirror behind the moment, the sober, heart-breaking record of guns and weary men, the ruins of deserted Richmond, delayed transports, and the faces of the generals,

Confederate and Federal. Although primarily of historic interest, Brady's plates have the esthetic overtone of naked, almost airless, factual truth, the distinction of suspended actuality, of objective immediacy not possible, even if desirable, in paint. Brady's work is an example of the camera's classic vision, austere and intense. The photographs by Brady, reproduced here, are typical of his sober and sensitive eye.

Unfortunately, few Americans followed in Brady's steps. Commercial photography, largely occupied with fashionable portraiture, descended to the decadence of flattery. People wanted to look beautiful and young. There was always the blessing of the retouching brush. But an even more sinister tendency was the attempt to make photographs imitate painting. Emphasis upon the qualities peculiar to photography were forgotten in the desire to imitate, in this less pretentious medium, the greater elegance of painted portrait or miniature. Photographs were judged on the basis of their resemblance to painting, not only in portrait photography but in outdoor pictures, where the atmospheric effects of certain nineteenth century painters were imitated increasingly as the century wore on, to the exclusion of all such direct purity as Brady's.

Eventually the photographer came to think of himself actually as a painter, or rather as master of an art parallel to painting, and of as great importance. By experimenting with sensitized papers, suppressing portions of the plate and accenting others, various fancy and "artistic" effects were achieved. Photographs came to look like etchings, like drawings, or like black-and-white reproductions of portraits by Whistler, Barbizon landscapes or the paintings of the Impressionists. In the example of soft-focus photography reproduced here, the influence of painting is obvious. Although it is the work of a splendid technician and has a charm of its own, interest in the effects of painting have dissolved the austere principles of the earlier and less sophisticated camera.

These "artistic" photographs were displayed widely in "salons," and had a remarkable popularity among amateurs, probably due partly to the commercialization of camera apparatus and accessories by astute manufacturers. Eventually, however, the salon idea provoked a healthy reaction. Through the efforts chiefly of Alfred Stieglitz and Edward Steichen, the one a brilliant photographer, the other a painter turned photographer, *Photo-Secession* was founded, and in 1903 *Camera Work*, the splendid quarterly magazine of the group, made its first appearance. With its magnificently reproduced plates, its distinguished editorial policy, and its interest in modern French painting, *Camera Work* did more than any other single force to elevate photography in America to its proper estate. One of the founders of *Camera Work* was Mrs. Gertrude Käsebier, the energetic wife of a Brooklyn brewer. Fashionable photographers of her day, such as Sarony, referred to her contemptuously as "that woman up the street," but they were jealous of her uptown clientele. She was much more than an amateur. She was a fine technician and she realized that photography was not painting but photography. Later, Clarence White, an Ohio business man whose avocation was photography, came on to New York and opened a school where many of our eminent contemporary photographers were trained.

Camera Work, however admirable in sum, was not free of the confusion concerning the esthetics of photography, though it made notable attempts by way of symposia and free discussion to clarify matters. The *Camera Work* group took themselves with the extreme seriousness of excellent craftsmen, but since they had to fight for the autonomy of photography, they were inclined to be over zealous as to the ultimate rôle of the camera. The art-photograph remained. It was a photograph to be sure, and no longer tried to imitate painting or etching, but it still played heavily on atmospheric effects and sentimentalized subjects. However, there was a definite revival of objective clarity as an ideal and a return to Brady's emphasis upon purely photographic means. The work of David Octavius Hill, the Scotch photographer, which was reproduced in *Camera Work,* had much to do with the revival of objective clarity.

The art-photographer exploits all the possibilities of lens and tripod with conscious choice. He may choose a simple object, the interest of which lies in the texture of the material of which it is composed, and make of that texture or surface quality the most important element of the picture. Edward Weston's photographs are good examples of this type of work. He may, as Steichen has done, choose a human face or other part of the body and by exaggeration or emphasis, concentration of light or massing of shadow, produce a portrait of symbolic characteristics—age, youth, nationality or even emotion. Or, he may take a familiar object, building or scene from a surprising or unfamiliar angle, a method which has been used by Alfred Stieglitz and by Charles Sheeler. (Stieglitz, the dean of American photographers, was one of the first to experiment with camera angles. A splendid technician, he gets in his work a very sensitive suggestion of textural quality and of the recession of planes in distance.) The moving picture camera, in most senses an entirely different development, has taught the still-photographer many dramatic uses. Then there are art-photographs of a slightly different nature, scenes of human interest caught in the passage of time and events, scenes which by their tragic or comic typicality summon up a whole world of related reference—a locomotive, the prow of an ocean liner, crowds in city streets, ferry boats, or architectural curiosities as keys to an epoch, seen in the photographs of Berenice Abbott, Walker Evans and Ralph Steiner. Close again to painting are the experiments of photographers who handle light as their paint, conceiving abstract patterns of some beauty by the employment of tonal values from black, through gray, to white in a purely arbitrary design. Man Ray and Francis Bruguière, not unaffected by the Cubists, have produced agreeable examples, which are, however, too small to be very decorative and too limited in scope to permit heroic enlargement.

Microphotography and the X-ray, though their real place is in the scientific laboratory, may also have a function in the realm of the purely decorative, providing us with patterns of germs, the symmetry of crystal, the architectural beauty of plant life, or the ghostly

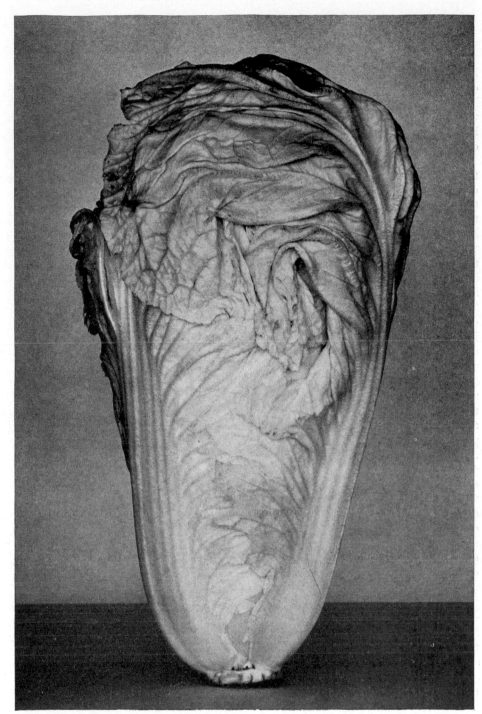

EDWARD WESTON
Chard

shadow of the light-penetrated organism. Color photography up to the present has been largely a question of the efficiency of various processes for color printing. It is unlikely that the invention of a universal process would alter the present basic conception of the function of the camera.

Recently the commercial uses of photography in America have been greatly extended. Photographs used as advertising posters were familiar as early as the nineties. Today the art-photograph has been made to serve all the uses of advertising, displacing original drawings to a very large extent. The camera lends itself admirably to advertising, reproducing alluringly the sheen of silk, the surface of an alligator pear, the cubic cleanliness of an electric refrigerator, in immaculate honesty. The element of the dramatic in photography has been used to great advantage. Advertisers have learned how to make spools of thread look like grain elevators and buttons like galaxies of moons. Fantasy in arrangement and lighting, well used, can provide the arresting quality necessary in advertising, and has resulted in a high grade of work. News photography is another interesting phase of commercial work. News photographs necessarily contain a very large element of the accidental. This accidental quality has been found to be very effective, and has been exploited to a considerable extent in the consciously accidental. Whether genuinely accidental or not, this type of picture often has a real interest as a social document, a fragment seized from its immediate context to satirize some phase of our life. Such shots have a surprising vitality, a breathing testimony,

EDWARD STEICHEN
GEORGE WASHINGTON BRIDGE (Photo-mural)

and sometimes an unflattering intimacy which many American periodicals show a tendency to exploit.

An interesting new development in photography is the photo-mural. The recent perfecting of large sheets of sensitized paper has made possible this use of enlarged photographs as wall decoration. But mere mechanical enlargement of a small picture does not make a photo-mural. The photographer, like the mural painter, must fit the scale of his mural to the wall space and make it harmonize with the surrounding architecture. The photo-mural has the advantage of greater speed and economy of execution over the work of the mural painter. For this reason, and probably because of the absence of color, architects today promise to be less timid about introducing photo-murals into their buildings than they are about painted mural decoration.

RALPH STEINER
AMERICAN RURAL BAROQUE

CHARLES SHEELER
FORD FACTORY

WALKER EVANS
SOUTH STREET, 1932

VI. The Motion Picture

By IRIS BARRY

THE MOTION picture is unique in three important ways. First, it is the one medium of expression in which America has influenced the rest of the world. Second, it has had a marked influence on contemporary life. And third, it is such a young art that we can study it at first hand from its beginnings: the primitives among movies are only forty years old.

Though many experiments and inventions had gone before, the motion picture as we know it did not come into being until, upon Eastman's inventing film to take the place of photographic plates, Edison perfected the kinetoscope. This peep-show machine made its first appearance at Broadway and 34th Street in New York in April, 1894. At first it was regarded only as a semi-scientific curiosity, even after other inventors had taken the animated pictures out of the peep-show and projected them on to a screen. For a time the public was satisfied merely to see things move. Scenic views, actual street scenes or simple actions—a woman dancing, an engine puffing towards the audience, a boy playing a prank—provided the subject-matter for these early movies. Little improvised comic or dramatic incidents were screened before the close of the nineteenth century, but very few attempts at sustained story-telling or drama were made until about 1903. In that year an Edison cameraman, Edwin S. Porter, combined several popular ingredients into a distinct plot in *The Great Train Robbery,* which was a whole reel long. Italy, France and England contributed many of the crude one-reel historical dramas, condensed plays and novels that followed, while America became identified with the livelier, more graphic and more purely cinematic cowboy dramas and slapstick comedies. Gradually films grew longer. The most famous of the early multi-reel movies was undoubtedly the French *Queen Elizabeth,* with Sarah Bernhardt, made in 1911.

In 1913 Italy sent over the super-spectacle *Quo Vadis,* complete with crowds, lions and the Colosseum in eight reels. D. W. Griffith, an ambitious young director who had then been with the American Biograph Co. for five years, determined to outdo *Quo Vadis.* The result was *The Birth of a Nation,* the film with which the history of the mo-

THE NEW YORK HAT, directed by D. W. Griffith about 1912. Mary Pickford and Lionel Barrymore in one of the close shots which Griffith introduced.

tion picture as a great popular art is usually judged to have begun. Griffith had already realized that the camera need not confine itself to action like that of the stage, with the players always seen at full-length at a constant distance from the spectator. He had already brought the camera closer to both actors and inanimate objects, and now found how to alternate more distant scenes of action with closer and more intimate scenes of emotion, making the film at once more fluid and expressive and less literal. He made dramatic use of the dissolve, the close-up and other technical tricks, and employed the old "ride to the rescue" motive of the early Western films, along with cutbacks, to achieve a contrapuntal method of pictorial narration. *The Birth of a Nation,* because of its magnitude as well as its subject and its treatment, and Griffith's colossal *Intolerance,* made two years later, had a lasting effect on the developing motion picture. It is noteworthy that *Intolerance,* perhaps the most momentous of all movies, was, like most of the interesting early American pictures, based on a story written specially for the screen and not on an adaptation of a novel or play.

From 1914 to 1918 the work of Grif-

CHARLIE, the tragi-comic figure created by Charles Chaplin.

SHANGHAI EXPRESS, directed by Josef von Sternberg, 1931. Modeled on a Soviet movie, "China Express."

LONE COWBOY, directed by Paul Sloan, 1933. The Western, one of America's most lively and typical contributions.

fith and others in America carried the movie out of the nickelodeon stage with its exaggerated gestures, rapid action and psychological crudity. It was during these years that Charlie Chaplin progressed from the rough-and-tumble farces of his beginnings to that brilliant succession of tragi-comedies which were tender and sardonic as well as funny, filled with a profound knowledge of human nature and assembled with an instinctive feeling for the medium. Both Griffith and Chaplin brought more complex situations and characters to the screen and taught it to find a purely visual expression unlike that of the drama or of fiction. Chaplin developed a sure feeling for the exact length of time each single shot should last: he, particularly, is a master of editing and of timing. Other men in this country made contributions, but many of them unhappily relied on famous stage actors, or on plots drawn unchanged from plays and novels, they too eagerly exploited sensationalism and personalities, and were more concerned with creating an impression of opulence than curious about the potentialities of the medium.

From the time filmgoers acclaimed the Biograph Girl with the golden curls, long before she was known as Mary Pickford, through to the time of Rudolph Valentino and Greta Garbo, the star system has done much to injure motion pictures. The great popular favorites themselves have all been exceptionally expressive players, but their popularity was abused when motion picture companies stressed who was in a movie rather than what was in it.

The years following the armistice brought technical innovations and an added sophistication from Germany. German films from the expressionist *Cabinet of Dr. Caligari* (1919) through to Dupont's *Variety* and Murnau's *The Last Laugh* (1925) left a marked impression. The use of camera angles and of the traveling camera, the designing of scenery for pictorial rather than for theatrical effect, both came from the German studios. It was the example of the Germans which influenced Hollywood to use artificial lighting as a rule rather than as an exception, and to construct artificial "outdoor" scenes within the studio in place of natural settings. With their slower movement, their exploration of somber moods and psychological bypaths the beautiful German films themselves were seldom to the public taste. But they were closely studied by American directors, and the innovations they presented were incorporated into the general technique of production, again widening the film's range of expression. During this period, many German directors, actors and cameramen were brought over to Hollywood.

The American movie on its own account had by no means stood still, despite the frankly commercial attitude of its makers. Cruze's *The Covered Wagon* (1923) was a far cry from the one-reel Westerns but was equally pure cinema. Erich von Stroheim's *Blind Husbands* (1919)—a remarkable piece—and his *Foolish Wives* (1922) were followed in 1923 by a movie which Chaplin directed but did not act in, *A Woman of Paris.* All three of these assumed a considerable degree of visual and intellectual alertness on the part of their audiences, and all of them contrived in a way, which at the time seemed startling, to suggest rather than to illustrate the finer shades of moods and of situations. Vivid and subtle as we found the American-made movies of the German director, Ernst Lubitsch—such, for instance as *The Marriage Circle* and *Forbidden Paradise*—their sparkle and eloquence had been foreshadowed in von Stroheim's and Chaplin's pictures.

In the years that followed, movies as different as Fairbanks' *The Black Pirate* in color, documentary pictures like *Chang, Moana* and *Tabu,* the farces of Harold Lloyd and Buster Keaton and the incomparable Chaplin's *The Pilgrim* and *The Gold Rush,* besides Ford's *The Iron Horse,* von Stroheim's *Greed,* Stiller's *Hotel Imperial* and Vidor's *The Big Parade* showed many indications of an intelligent struggle to explore the screen's possibilities.

In 1928 with the appearance of *The Jazz Singer* every motion picture studio set about making talkies. The movies had achieved a remarkable degree of eloquence through pictures alone. There was a temporary setback with the coming of audible dialogue. Canned plays threatened to sweep away most of the advances made by the silent films. It is well to remember, however, that except in unusual productions like Chaplin's *The Woman of Paris* and Murnau's *The Last Laugh,* one third of the footage of the average silent film consisted of printed subtitles. Silent films, too, were invariably accompanied by both music and sound effects from the theater orchestra.

By 1929 talkies like Victor Fleming's outdoor *The Virginian* and von Sternberg's German-made *The Blue Angel* succeeded in shaking off the restrictions at first imposed by the mechanics of sound-recording. A French movie, René Clair's *Sous les Toits de Paris,* indicated to what an extent intelligently used sound could become an asset. The screen quickly regained its range and wealth of pictorial expression, dialogue became briefer, less continuous and more natural. In the brilliantly edited Mickey Mouse and Silly Symphonies, the animated cartoons equipped with sound have shown a new vitality and inventiveness beyond that displayed by other branches of the art.

The influence of many remarkable films made in Soviet Russia has not been very marked. The Russian directors, of whom Pudovkin and Eisenstein are best known, avowedly derive in part from D. W. Griffith. With a metronomic, machine-gun fire of rapid and realistic shots (usually close-ups) in place of the customary sustained scenes, they have achieved in almost physical intensity of expression. The present tendency to choose players physically well-suited to interpret each part rather than established favorites may well be due to them. But their influence in this country was more noticeable in an increase of productions with a sociological flavor, such as *I Am a Fugitive from the Chain Gang* and *Wild Boys of the Road*.

The many types of films—documentary, spectacular, historical, Western, comedy-drama, slapstick, animated cartoon—were established in the early days of the cinema. Not a single type has yet been fully developed, though recent years have seen considerable advances both in photography, decor and acting and three or four notable extensions in the technical use of the medium. From the first, progress has been retarded by the necessity for producing companies to entertain their immense public, their consequent neglect to explore the innate possibilities of the film itself and their insistence on proven ingredients and glamorous personalities. Almost all purely experimental movies have been the work of amateurs—painters like Charles Sheeler, Fernand Léger, Viking Eggeling, Salvador Dali (on whose scenario the striking surrealist movie *L'Age d'Or* was based) Jean Cocteau with his surrealist *Le Sang d'un Poète*, or Melville Webber and Dr. Watson whose *Fall of the House of Usher* and *Lot in Sodom* are among the most interesting non-commercial films made in this country. Very seldom, as with *The Cabinet of Dr. Caligari* and Chaplin's *A Woman of Paris*, and then only under special conditions have experimental films been made within the industry itself.

Another grave detriment has been the passing of almost all motion picture theaters into the hands of the producing companies, so that mass-produced films are automatically poured out through chain-store theaters. The result is necessarily mediocre, as though all book publishers and booksellers strove to issue nothing but best sellers. Good films are produced and are sometimes overwhelmingly successful, whether nationally advertised as is usual with superfilms good or bad, or whether brought back time and again by popular demand. Others however, and those often the most vital and original, are shown only in a fugitive way to small and often the wrong audiences, or cannot find an outlet at all.

Much could be done to remedy this state of affairs by organization on the part of discontented filmgoers. It has been proved that active local demand can dictate what shall be shown in neighborhood houses. Much could also be done by discriminating film fans with letters written to producing companies and to cinemas. These would not be disregarded. Unfortunately, it is usually the undiscriminating and not the critical filmgoers who write letters. Nevertheless, it is undoubtedly in the hands of the few creative directors and of the general public that the future of this great twentieth century art still lies. They will determine whether it shall remain as now largely a diversion in which mere photography and secondhand theater play all too large a part, or whether it shall develop fully its unique methods of expression.

BLIND HUSBANDS, directed by Erich von Stroheim, 1919. Precursor of a school of sophisticated comedy. Emphasis on the dramatic significance of objects—the edelweiss in the feminine shoe.

MOANA, directed by Robert Flaherty in the South Sea Islands, 1926. Magnificent photography and the clever use of native characters in a documentary movie.

LOT IN SODOM, directed by J. S. Watson, Jr. and Melville Webber, 1934. An experimental sound-film. Pictorial values stressed rather than story.

LIST OF ARTISTS AND LOCATION OF THEIR WORK

A LIST of artists and of the places where their works may be found. The list is not exhaustive. Names of cities without symbols indicate the art museum of that city. For example, the name Chicago refers to the Art Institute of Chicago. Where symbols follow the name of a city, specific museums in that city are indicated, for instance, New York (MM, MMA, WM) means that the artist is represented in The Metropolitan Museum, The Museum of Modern Art and the Whitney Museum of American Art.

EXPLANATION OF SYMBOLS

AA—Ann Arbor Art Association.
AGAA—Addison Gallery of American Art.
AI—Art Institute.
BM—Brooklyn Museum.
CAA—Carolina Art Association.
CGA—Corcoran Gallery of Art.
CPLH—California Palace of the Legion of Honor.
CU—Cooper Union.
FGA—Freer Gallery of Art.
GLA—Gallery of Living Art.
ISGM—Isabella Stewart Gardner Museum.
LAG—Layton Art Gallery.
MA—San Francisco Museum of Art.
MAG—Davenport Municipal Art Gallery.
MFA—Museum of Fine Arts.
MM—Metropolitan Museum of Art.
MMA—Museum of Modern Art.
NAC—National Arts Club.
NAD—National Academy of Design.
NGA—National Gallery of Art.
NYPL—New York Public Library.
PAFA—Pennsylvania Academy of the Fine Arts.
PI—Peabody Institute.
PM—Davenport Public Museum.
PMA—Pennsylvania Museum of Art.
PMG—Phillips Memorial Gallery.
RM—Roerich Museum.
SMFA—Springfield Museum of Fine Arts.
UM—University Museum.
UW—University of Washington.
WAMM—Wadsworth Atheneum and Morgan Memorial.
WM—Whitney Museum of American Art.
WRN—William Rockhill Nelson Gallery.

GEORGE C. AULT, 1891-
Los Angeles, Newark, New York (WM).
PEGGY BACON, 1895-
New York (MM, MMA, WM).
GEORGE GREY BARNARD, 1863-
Chicago, New York (MM, Lincoln School), Pittsburgh. Monuments: State Capitol, Harrisburg, Pa.; *Lincoln*, Cincinnati, Louisville, Ky., Manchester, England; *The Hewer*, Cairo, Ill.
GIFFORD BEAL, 1879-
Chicago, Cleveland, Denver, Detroit, Los Angeles, Merion, Pa. (Barnes Found.), Newark, New York (BM, MM, WM), San Francisco (MA), Savannah, Ga., Syracuse, N. Y., Washington, D. C. (CGA, PMG).
GEORGE BELLOWS, 1882-1925
Andover, Mass. (AGAA), Boston (MFA), Buffalo, Chicago, Cincinnati, Cleveland, Columbus, Ohio, Detroit, Los Angeles, Minneapolis, Newark, New York (BM, MM, WM), Philadelphia (PAFA), Pittsburgh, Provi-

dence, San Diego, Savannah, Ga., Toledo, Washington, D. C. (CGA, PMG), Worcester.
THOMAS BENTON, 1889-
Murals: New York (New School for Social Research, Whitney Museum), Indiana Building at Century of Progress, Chicago (to be permanently placed by State of Indiana).
RALPH ALBERT BLAKELOCK, 1847-1919
Andover, Mass. (AGAA), Buffalo, Cincinnati, Cleveland, Davenport, Ia. (MAG), Manchester, N. H., Milwaukee (LAG), Montclair, N. J., Muskegon, Mich., New York (BM, MM, WM), Northampton, Mass., Pittsburgh, Pittsfield, Mass., Washington, D. C. (CGA, NGA), Worcester.
PETER BLUME, 1906-
Columbus, Ohio, New York (WM).
ALEXANDER BROOK, 1898-
Ann Arbor, Mich. (AA), Buffalo, Chicago, Detroit, New York (GLA, MM, WM), Pittsburgh, St. Louis, San Francisco (CPLH).
HENRY KIRKE BROWN, 1814-1886
New York (MM, Church of the Annunciation, N. Y. Historical Society, *Washington* and *Lincoln* in Union Sq., Prospect Pk. and Greenwood Cemetery, Brooklyn), Washington, D. C. (National Statuary Hall, etc.)
CHARLES BURCHFIELD, 1893-
Buffalo, Cambridge, Mass., Cleveland, Columbus, Ohio, Indianapolis, Newark, New York (BM, MM, MMA, WM).
MARY CASSATT, 1845-1927
Andover, Mass. (AGAA), Boston (MFA), Cambridge, Mass., Chicago, Cincinnati, Cleveland, Detroit, Hartford (WAMM), Indianapolis, Los Angeles, Newark, New York (MM), Philadelphia (PMA), Providence, Washington, D. C. (CGA, NGA), Worcester.
WILLIAM MERRITT CHASE, 1849-1916
Boston (MFA), Buffalo, Chicago, Cincinnati, Cleveland, Davenport, Ia. (MAG), Detroit, Fort Worth, Tex., Hartford (WAMM), Houston, Tex., Indianapolis, Los Angeles, New York (BM, MM), Northampton, Mass., Philadelphia (PAFA), Pittsburgh, Providence, San Antonio, Tex., Savannah, Ga., Seattle (UW), Toledo, Washington, D. C. (CGA, NGA).
GLENN O. COLEMAN, 1887-1932
Newark, New York (BM, GLA, WM), Washington, D. C. (PMG).
ALFRED Q. COLLINS, 1855-1903
Boston (MFA), New York (BM, MM)
JOHN STEUART CURRY, 1897-
New York (WM).
ANDREW DASBURG, 1887-
Los Angeles, New York (WM).
JO DAVIDSON, 1883-
New York (WM, Columbia Univ., Mt. Sinai Hospital, Neighborhood Playhouse Studios, Paramount Theater, Standard Oil Co. Bldg.), Paris (American Embassy), Urbana, Ill.
ARTHUR B. DAVIES, 1862-1928
Andover, Mass. (AGAA), Chicago, Cincinnati, Cleveland, Columbus, Ohio, Detroit, Hartford (WAMM), Indianapolis, Los Angeles, Minneapolis, Montclair, N. J., Newark, New Britain, Conn., New Orleans, New York (BM, MM, MMA, WM), Philadelphia (Art Club, PMA), Pittsburgh, Portland, Ore., Providence, Rochester, San Diego, San Francisco (MA), Savannah, Ga., Utica (Public Library), Washington, D. C. (CGA, PMG), Worcester, Youngstown, Ohio. Murals: New York (International House).
STUART DAVIS, 1894-
Los Angeles, Newark, New York (WM), Philadelphia (PAFA), Washington, D. C. (PMG).

CHARLES DEMUTH, 1883-
Cambridge, Mass., Chicago, Cleveland, Columbus, Ohio, Hartford (WAMM), Los Angeles, Merion, Pa. (Barnes Found.), New York (BM, GLA, MM, WM), Rochester, Washington, D. C. (PMG).
THOMAS WILMER DEWING, 1851-
Andover, Mass. (AGAA), Buffalo, Chicago, New York (BM, MM), Pittsburgh, Providence, St. Louis, Toledo, Washington, D. C. (CGA, FGA, NGA, PMG).
PRESTON DICKINSON, 1891-1930
Cambridge, Mass., Cincinnati, Cleveland, Columbus, Ohio, Detroit, Hartford (WAMM), Los Angeles, Newark, New York (BM, GLA, MMA, WM), Northampton, Mass., Omaha, Neb., Philadelphia (PAFA), Washington, D. C. (PMG).
HUNT DIEDERICH, 1884-
Newark, New York (MM, WM).
ARTHUR G. DOVE, 1880-
Columbus, Ohio, Washington, D. C. (PMG)
GUY PÈNE DuBOIS, 1884-
Los Angeles, Newark, New York (MM), Washington, D. C. (PMG).
FRANK DUVENECK, 1848-1919
Andover, Mass. (AGAA), Atlanta, Ga., Boston (MFA), Buffalo, Chicago, Cincinnati, Cleveland, Columbus, Ohio, Fort Worth, Tex., Hartford (WAMM), Indianapolis, Philadelphia (PAFA), Toledo, Washington, D. C. (NGA).
THOMAS EAKINS, 1844-1916
Andover, Mass. (AGAA), Boston (MFA), Chicago, Cleveland, Detroit, Fort Worth, Tex., Los Angeles, Merion, Pa. (Barnes Found.), New Haven, New York (BM, MM, NAD, WM), Northampton, Mass., Philadelphia (Jefferson Medical College, PAFA, PMA, UM), Pittsburgh, Washington, D. C. (CGA, PMG).
LOUIS EILSHEMIUS, 1864-
Cleveland, Detroit, New York (MM, WM), Washington, D. C. (PMG).
JACOB EPSTEIN, 1880-
Buffalo, Chicago, Cincinnati, Newark, New York (BM, MM, MMA), Northampton, Mass. Monuments: Sculptures on London Underground Building; Memorial to W. H. Hudson, Hyde Park, London; Tomb of Oscar Wilde, Père Lachaise Cemetery, Paris.
ERNEST FIENE, 1894-
Boston, Chicago, Detroit, Los Angeles, Newark, New York (NYPL, WM), Pittsburgh, San Francisco (CPLH), Washington, D. C. (PMG).
ARNOLD FRIEDMAN, 1879-
Newark, New York (MMA).
GEORGE FULLER, 1822-1884
Andover, Mass. (AGAA), Chicago, Cleveland, Kansas City (WRN), New York (MM), Northampton, Mass., St. Louis, Toledo, Washington, D. C. (NGA, PMG), Worcester.
EMIL GANSO, 1895-
Cleveland, Denver, Houston, Tex., Los Angeles, New York (MM, WM, NYPL), Portland, Ore., Worcester.
WILLIAM J. GLACKENS, 1870-
Chicago, Columbus, Ohio, Detroit, Los Angeles, Minneapolis, Newark, New York (MM, WM), Washington, D. C. (PMG).
ANNE GOLDTHWAITE
Baltimore, Chicago, Cleveland, Montgomery, Ala., New York (BM, NYPL), Washington, D. C. (Library of Congress).
SAMUEL HALPERT, 1884-1930
Cleveland, Detroit, Los Angeles, Newark, New York (WM), Philadelphia (PAFA), San

Francisco (CPLH), Washington, D. C. (PMG).

GEORGE OVERBURY (POP) HART, 1868-1933
Chicago, Cincinnati, Cleveland, Los Angeles, Newark, New York (BM, MM, NYPL), Washington, D. C. (NGA).

MARSDEN HARTLEY, 1878-
Cleveland, Columbus, Ohio, New York (WM), Washington, D. C. (PMG).

CHILDE HASSAM, 1859-
Andover, Mass. (AGAA), Boston (MFA), Buffalo, Chicago, Cincinnati, Detroit, Easthampton, L. I., Hagerstown, Md., Indianapolis, Los Angeles, Milwaukee (AI), Minneapolis, Montclair, N. J., Newark, New York (BM, MM), Northampton, Mass., Philadelphia (PAFA), Pittsburgh, Providence, St. Louis, Savannah, Ga., Seattle (UW), Syracuse, N. Y., Toledo, Washington, D. C. (CGA, FGA, NGA, PMG), Worcester.

ROBERT HENRI, 1865-1929
Boston (MFA), Buffalo, Charleston, S. C. (CAA), Chicago, Cincinnati, Columbus, Ohio, Dallas, Tex., Decatur, Ill., Des Moines, Detroit, Kansas City (AI), Lawrence, Kan., Los Angeles, Memphis, Tenn., Montclair, N. J., Newark, New Orleans, New York (BM, MM, NAC, WM), Oberlin, Ohio, Philadelphia (PAFA), Pittsburgh, Providence, Rochester, St. Louis, San Diego, San Francisco (MA), Santa Fe, N. M., Savannah, Ga., Spartanburg, S. C., Toledo, Washington, D. C. (CGA, PMG), Youngstown, Ohio.

STEFAN HIRSCH, 1899-
Cleveland, Los Angeles, Newark, New York (WM), Washington, D. C. (PMG), Worcester.

WINSLOW HOMER, 1836-1910
Andover, Mass. (AGAA), Baltimore (PI), Boston (MFA), Cambridge, Mass., Chicago, Cincinnati, Cleveland, Detroit, Hartford (WAMM), Indianapolis, Laurel, Miss., Lawrence, Kan., Manchester, N. H., Milwaukee (LAG), Muskegon, Mich., New York (BM, CU, MM, WM), Northampton, Mass., Philadelphia (PAFA), Pittsburgh, Providence, San Diego, Seattle (UW), Toledo, Washington, D. C. (CGA, FGA, NGA, PMG), Worcester, Youngstown, Ohio.

EDWARD HOPPER, 1882-
Cambridge, Mass., Chicago, Cleveland, Hartford (WAMM), Indianapolis, New Orleans, New York (BM, MM, MMA, NYPL, WM), Philadelphia (PAFA), Washington, D. C. (PMG).

WILLIAM MORRIS HUNT, 1824-1879
Boston (MFA), Buffalo, Indianapolis, New York (MM), Philadelphia (PAFA), Toledo, Worcester.

GEORGE INNESS, 1825-1894
Andover, Mass. (AGAA), Baltimore (PI), Boston (MFA), Buffalo, Chicago, Cincinnati, Cleveland, Davenport, Ia. (MAG), Detroit, Fort Worth, Tex., Hartford (WAMM), Houston, Tex., Indianapolis, Lawrence, Kan., Kansas City (WRN), Manchester, N. H., Milwaukee (LAG), Minneapolis, Montclair, N. J., Montreal, New York (BM, MM), Northampton, Mass., Pittsburgh, Pittsfield, Mass., St. Louis, Seattle (UW), Toledo, Washington, D. C. (CGA, NGA, PMG), Worcester.

MORRIS KANTOR, 1896-
Chicago, New York (GLA, WM), Philadelphia (PAFA), Washington, D. C. (PMG).

BERNARD KARFIOL, 1886-
Detroit, Los Angeles, Newark, New York (MM, MMA, WM), San Francisco (CPLH), Washington, D. C. (CGA, PMG).

HENRY G. KELLER, 1870-
Cambridge, Mass., Cleveland, Washington, D. C. (PMG).

ROCKWELL KENT, 1882-
Chicago, Cleveland, Columbus, Ohio, Houston, Tex., Indianapolis, Minneapolis, New York (BM, MM, RM, WM), Pittsburgh, Washington, D. C. (NGA, PMG).

WALT KUHN, 1880-
Andover, Mass. (AGAA), Chicago, Los Angeles, New York (BM, MMA, WM), San Francisco (CPLH), Washington, D. C. (PMG).

YASUO KUNIYOSHI, 1893-
Columbus, Ohio, New York (GLA, WM). Mural: Rockefeller Center Music Hall.

GASTON LACHAISE, 1882-
Cleveland, Hartford (WAMM), Newark, New London, New York (MMA, WM), Northampton, Mass., Philadelphia (PMA), Washington, D. C. (PMG). Monuments and architectural sculpture: Chicago (Century of Progress), New York (Rockefeller Center, Amer. Tel. & Tel. Bldg.), Washington, D. C. (Nat'l. Coast Guard Memorial, Arlington).

JOHN LA FARGE, 1835-1910.
Andover, Mass. (AGAA), Boston (MFA), Cambridge, Mass., Cincinnati, Cleveland, Los Angeles, New York (MM, WM), Northampton, Mass., St. Louis, Washington, D. C. (NGA, PMG), Worcester. Murals and windows: Baltimore (Courthouse), Boston (Trinity Church), Buffalo (Trinity Church), Cambridge (Memorial Hall, Harvard Univ.), New York, (Church of the Ascension, Church of the Paulist Fathers, St. Paul's Chapel of Columbia Univ.), St. Paul (Minnesota Capitol).

ROBERT LAURENT, 1890-
Chicago, Merion, Pa. (Barnes Found.), Newark, New York (BM, RM, WM, Rockefeller Center Music Hall).

ERNEST LAWSON, 1873-
Chicago, Columbus, Ohio, Los Angeles, Milwaukee (AI), Montclair, N. J., Newark, New York (BM, MM, WM), St. Louis, San Francisco (CPLH), Savannah, Ga., Washington, D. C. (CGA, NGA, PMG), Worcester, Youngstown, Ohio.

ARTHUR LEE, 1891-
New York (BM, MM, WM).

GEORGE LUKS, 1867-1933
Andover, Mass. (AGAA), Buffalo, Cleveland, Columbus, Ohio, Detroit, Los Angeles, Merion, Pa. (Barnes Found.), Milwaukee (AI), Newark, New Haven, New Orleans, New York (MM, WM), Pittsburgh, Providence, Washington, D. C. (CGA, PMG).

HENRY LEE McFEE, 1886-
Ann Arbor, Mich. (AA), Buffalo, Cleveland, Columbus, Ohio, Detroit, New York (BM, MM, WM), Springfield, Mass. (SMFA), Washington, D. C. (CGA, PMG).

PAUL MANSHIP, 1885-
Andover, Mass. (AGAA), Cambridge, Mass., Chicago, Cincinnati, Cleveland, Detroit, Indianapolis, Minneapolis, Milwaukee (AI), Newark, New York (BM, MM, Pratt Inst.), Northampton, Mass., St. Louis, Toledo, Washington, D. C. (CGA). Monuments: Andover, Mass., Detroit, Fort Wayne, Ind., New York (Rockefeller Center, Bronx Park), Philadelphia, St. Paul.

JOHN MARIN, 1870-
Cambridge, Mass., Chicago, Cleveland, Columbus, Ohio, Los Angeles, Newark, New York (BM, GLA, MM, WM), Rochester, San Francisco (MA), Washington, D. C. (PMG).

REGINALD MARSH, 1898-
New York (MM, WM).

HOMER DODGE MARTIN, 1898-
Albany (Inst. of History & Art), Andover, Mass. (AGAA), Chicago, Cleveland, Davenport, Ia. (MAG), Hartford (WAMM), Kan-

sas City (AI), Lawrence, Kan., Montclair, N. J., New York (BM, MM), Pittsburgh, Pittsfield, Mass., St. Louis, Seattle (UW), Washington, D. C. (NGA).

ALFRED H. MAURER, 1868-1932
Merion, Pa. (Barnes Found.), Philadelphia (PMA), Washington, D. C. (PMG).

KENNETH HAYES MILLER, 1876-
Cleveland, Columbus, Ohio, Los Angeles, New York (MM, MMA, WM), Washington, D. C. (PMG).

JEROME MYERS, 1867-
Chicago, Columbus, Ohio, Los Angeles, Milwaukee (AI), Newark, New York (MM, WM), Savannah, Ga., Washington, D. C. (PMG).

REUBEN NAKIAN, 1897-
Newark, New York (MMA, WM).

ISAMU NOGUCHI, 1904-
Buffalo, New York (WM).

GEORGIA O'KEEFFE, 1887-
Cambridge, Mass., Cleveland, Merion, Pa. (Barnes Found.), New York, (MM, WM), Washington, D. C. (PMG).

JOSEPH POLLET, 1897-
Los Angeles, Newark, New York (GLA, WM), Washington, D. C. (PMG).

HENRY VARNUM POOR, 1888-
Chicago, New York (MM, WM), Worcester. Ceramic ceilings: New York (Rockefeller Center, Union Dime Savings Bank).

MAURICE PRENDERGAST, 1861-1924
Andover, Mass. (AGAA), Boston (MFA), Cleveland, Columbus, Ohio, Detroit, Los Angeles, Merion, Pa. (Barnes Found.), New York (WM), Washington, D. C. (PMG).

FREDERICK REMINGTON, 1861-1909
New York (MM), Ogdensburg, N. Y. (Remington Art Memorial), Toledo, Washington, D. C. (NGA). Monuments: Philadelphia (*Cowboy*, Fairmount Pk.)

WILLIAM RIMMER, 1816-1879
Boston (Art Club, MFA), New York (MM).

BOARDMAN ROBINSON, 1876-
Newark, New York (WM). Murals: New York (Rockefeller Center), Pittsburgh (Kaufmann Dep't Store).

THEODORE ROBINSON, 1852-1896
Atlanta, Ga., Columbus, Ohio, Lawrence, Kan., Montclair, N. J., New York (MM, WM), Northampton, Mass., Washington, D. C. (CGA, NGA, PMG).

JOHN ROGERS, 1829-1904
Newark, New York (N. Y. Hist. Soc.), Philadelphia (*General Reynolds*).

ALBERT PINKHAM RYDER, 1847-1917
Akron, Ohio, Andover, Mass. (AGAA), Boston (MFA), Buffalo, Cambridge, Mass., Chicago, Cleveland, Columbus, Ohio, Detroit, Minneapolis, Montclair, N. J., New York (BM, MM, WM), Northampton, Mass., Rochester, St. Louis, San Diego, Toledo, Washington, D. C. (FGA, NGA, PMG), Worcester, Youngstown, Ohio.

AUGUSTUS SAINT-GAUDENS, 1848-1907
Boston (MFA), Buffalo, Chicago, Cleveland, Detroit, Indianapolis, Los Angeles, Newark, New Haven, New York (MM, MM, WM), Philadelphia (PMA), Pittsburgh, St. Louis, Washington, D. C. (CGA). Monuments: Boston (*Shaw Memorial*), Chicago (*Lincoln*), New York (*Farragut, Peter Cooper, General Sherman*), Philadelphia (*Garfield, Samuel Chapin-Puritan*), Springfield, Mass. (*Samuel Chapin*), Washington (*Adams Memorial, Rock Creek Cemetery*).

JOHN SINGER SARGENT, 1856-1925
Andover, Mass. (AGAA), Boston (ISGM, MFA), Buffalo, Cambridge, Mass., Chicago, Cincinnati, Cleveland, Detroit, Hartford

(WAMM), Indianapolis, New York (BM, MM), Northampton, Mass., Philadelphia (PAFA, PMA), Providence, Toledo, Washington, D. C. (CGA, FGA, NGA).

CHARLES SHEELER, 1883-
Cambridge, Mass., Chicago, Cleveland, Columbus, Ohio, New York (GLA, WM), Springfield (SMFA), Washington, D. C. (PMG).

JOHN SLOAN, 1871-
Chicago, Cincinnati, Detroit, Los Angeles, Merion, Pa. (Barnes Found.), Newark, New York (BM, MM, NYPL, WM), Pittsburgh, San Diego, Santa Fe, N. M., State College, Pa., Washington, D. C. (PMG).

EUGENE SPEICHER, 1883-
Andover, Mass. (AGAA), Buffalo, Cambridge, Mass., Cincinnati, Cleveland, Decatur, Ill., Des Moines, Detroit, Galveston, Tex., Minneapolis, New Haven, New York (BM, MM, WM), Omaha, Pittsburgh, Providence, St. Louis, San Francisco (CPLH), Washington, D. C. (CGA, NGA, PMG).

NILES SPENCER, 1893-
Buffalo, Columbus, Ohio, Newark, New York (WM), Washington, D. C. (PMG).

JOSEPH STELLA, 1880-
New York (WM).

MAURICE STERNE, 1877-
Andover, Mass. (AGAA), Boston (MFA), Cambridge, Mass., Chicago, Cleveland, Detroit, Los Angeles, New York (BM, MM, WM), Northampton, Mass., Pittsburgh, Providence, St. Louis, San Diego, San Francisco (CPLH), Washington, D. C. (CGA, PMG), Worcester. Monument to the Early Settlers, Worcester.

ABBOTT HANDERSON THAYER, 1849-1921
Andover, Mass. (AGAA), Boston (MFA), Buffalo, Cincinnati, Cleveland, Dayton, Ohio, Indianapolis, Milwaukee (LAG), New York (MM), Northampton, Mass., Providence, Washington, D. C. (FGA, NGA), Worcester. Mural: Brunswick, Me. (Bowdoin College).

JOHN H. TWACHTMAN, 1853-1902
Andover, Mass. (AGAA), Boston (ISGM, MFA), Buffalo, Chicago, Cincinnati, Daven-

port, Ia. (MAG), Hagerstown, Md., Indianapolis, Kansas City (WRN), Minneapolis, Montclair, N. J., New York (MM, WM), Northampton, Mass., Pittsburgh, Washington, D. C. (FGA, NGA, PMG).

ABRAHAM WALKOWITZ, 1880-
Los Angeles, Newark, New York (WM), Washington, D. C. (PMG).

CARL WALTERS, 1883-
Alfred, N. Y., Chicago, Davenport, Ia. (MAG), New York (MM, WM), Portland, Ore., Worcester.

JOHN QUINCY ADAMS WARD, 1830-1910
Monuments: *Good Samaritan*, Publ. Garden, Boston; *Lafayette*, Burlington, Vt.; *William Gilmore Simms*, Charleston, S. C.; *General Reynolds*, Gettysburg, Pa.; *Israel Putnam* and Statues in Capitol, Hartford; *Washington*, Newburyport, Mass.; *Commodore Perry*, Newport, R. I.; in New York:—*Shakespeare, Indian Hunter, Pilgrim, Seventh Regiment Memorial*, Central Pk.; *Washington*, Sub-Treasury Bldg.; Pediment of New York Stock Exchange; *William Dodge,* Herald Sq.; *Horace Greeley*, Tribune Bldg.; *Alexander Lyman Holley*, Wash. Sq.; *Henry Ward Beecher*, Brooklyn; *Naval Victory*, Dewey Arch; *Roscoe Conkling*, Madison Sq.; *General Hancock*, Fairmount Pk., Philadelphia; Library, St. Johnsbury, Vt., *General Daniel Morgan*, Spartanburg, S. C.; *Soldiers and Sailors Monument*, Syracuse, N. Y.; *General Thomas* and *Garfield Monument*, Washington, D. C.

OLIN LEVI WARNER, 1844-1896
Boston (*William Lloyd Garrison*), New York (MM, *Fountains*—Central Park and Union Square), Portland, Ore. (*Fountain*), Washington, D. C. (*Doors*—Library of Congress).

FRANKLIN C. WATKINS, 1890-
New York (WM), Philadelphia (PAFA). Murals: Philadelphia (Rodin Museum).

HARRY W. WATROUS, 1857-
Buffalo, Fort Worth, Tex., Montpelier, Vt., New York (BM, MM), Portland, Me., St. Louis, Washington, D. C. (CGA).

MAX WEBER, 1881-
Cleveland, Columbus, Ohio, Detroit, Los An-

geles, Newark, New York (BM, GLA, MM, WM), Washington, D. C. (PMG).

J. ALDEN WEIR, 1852-1919
Andover, Mass. (AGAA), Buffalo, Chicago, Cleveland, Davenport, Ia. (MAG), Detroit, Indianapolis, Montclair, N. J., New York (BM, MM, WM), Northampton, Mass., Philadelphia (PAFA), Pittsburgh, Providence, Seattle (UW), Syracuse, N. Y., Washington, D. C. (CGA, NGA, PMG), Worcester.

JAMES ABBOTT McNEILL WHISTLER, 1834-1903
Andover, Mass. (AGAA), Baltimore, Boston (ISGM, MFA), Cambridge, Mass., Chicago, Cincinnati, Cleveland, Detroit, Farmington, Conn., Haverford, Pa., Kansas City (WRN), Muskegon, Mich., New Haven, New York (BM, MM), Northampton, Mass., Philadelphia (PMA), Pittsburgh, Providence, Syracuse, N. Y., Toledo, Washington, D. C. (FGA, NGA, PMG), Worcester. Foreign Museums: Amsterdam, Dublin, Glasgow, Honolulu, London, Paris.

GERTRUDE VANDERBILT WHITNEY
New York (WM). Monuments: Montreal (*Fountain*, McGill Univ.), New York (*Mitchell Memorial*), Washington, D. C. (*Titanic Memorial*).

ALEXANDER H. WYANT, 1836-1892
Andover, Mass. (AGAA), Chicago, Cincinnati, Cleveland, Davenport, Ia. (MAG), Detroit, Hartford (WAMM), Manchester, N. H., Milwaukee (LAG), Montclair, N. J., New York (MM, WM), Northampton, Mass., Pittsburgh, Pittsfield, Mass., St. Louis, Seattle (UW), Toledo, Washington, D. C. (CGA, NGA), Worcester.

WILLIAM ZORACH, 1887-
Chicago, Columbus, Ohio, Los Angeles, Newark, New York (BM, WM, Rockefeller Center Music Hall), Washington, D. C. (PMG).

Works by many other contemporary artists mentioned in the articles on painting and sculpture but not included in this list may be found in The Metropolitan Museum, The Brooklyn Museum, the Whitney Museum of American Art, all in New York, the Carnegie Institute in Pittsburgh, The Art Institute of Chicago.

BIBLIOGRAPHY—PAINTERS AND SCULPTORS—GENERAL

ADAMS, ADELINE, The Spirit of American Sculpture. *New York, The National Sculpture Society*, 1929.

BARKER, VIRGIL, A Critical Introduction to American Painting. *New York, Whitney Museum of American Art*, 1931.

BIRNBAUM, MARTIN, Introductions; painters, sculptors and graphic artists. *New York, Frederic Fairchild Sherman*, 1919.

BLASHFIELD, EDWIN HOWLAND, Mural Painting in America. *New York, Charles Scribner's Sons*, 1913.

CAFFIN, CHARLES HENRY, American Masters of Painting. *New York, Doubleday, Page & Company*, 1906.

— — —The Story of American Painting. *New York, Frederick A. Stokes Company*, 1907.

— — —American Masters of Sculpture. *New York, Doubleday, Page & Company*, 1903.

CORTISSOZ, ROYAL, American Artists. *New York and London, Charles Scribner's Sons*, 1923.

FIELDING, MANTLE, Dictionary of American Painters, Sculptors, and Engravers. *Philadelphia, Lancaster Press, Inc.*, 1926.

GALLATIN, ALBERT EUGENE, American Water-Colourists. *New York, E. P. Dutton & Company*, 1922.

GUTHRIE, ANNA LORRAINE, American Art; a Study Outline. *White Plains, N. Y. and New York City, H. W. Wilson Company*, 1917.

HARSHE, ROBERT BARTHOLOW, A Reader's Guide to Modern Art, *San Francisco*, 1914.

HARTMANN, SADAKICHI, History of American Art, *Boston*, 1901. Revised edition, 1934.

ISHAM, SAMUEL, The History of American Painting. *New York, The Macmillan Company*, 1927.

JEWELL, EDWARD ALDEN, Americans. *New York, Alfred A. Knopf*, 1930.

KOOTZ, SAMUEL M., Modern American Painters. *New York, Brewer & Warren, Inc.*, 1930.

LaFOLLETTE, SUZANNE, Art in America. *New York and London, Harper and Brothers*, 1929.

McSPADDEN, J. WALKER, Famous Painters of America. *New York, Dodd, Mead & Company*, 1923.

— — —Famous Sculptors of America. *New York, Dodd, Mead & Company*, 1924.

MATHER, FRANK JEWETT and MOREY, CHARLES RUFUS, The American Spirit in Art, Vol. 12, The Pageant of America series. *New Haven, Yale University Press*, 1927.

MUMFORD, LEWIS, The Brown Decades; a Study of the Arts in America, 1865-1895. *New York, Harcourt, Brace & Company*, 1931.

MURRELL, WILLIAM, A History of American Graphic Humor. *New York, Whitney Museum of American Art*, 1934.

NEUHAUS, EUGEN, The History and Ideals of American Art. *Palo Alto, Cal., Stanford University Press*, 1931.

PACH, WALTER, Modern Art in America. *New York, C. W. Kraushaar Art Galleries*, 1928.

PHILLIPS, DUNCAN, A Collection in the Making. Washington, Phillips Memorial Gallery. *New York, E. Weyhe*, 1926.

POST, CHANDLER RATHFON, A History of European and American Sculpture, from the Early Christian Period to the Present Day; vol. II, chap. XXIX and XXX. *Cambridge, Harvard University Press*, 1921.

POUSETTE-DART, NATHANIEL, Distinguished American Artists. *New York*, 1922.

SMITH, F. HOPKINSON, American Illustrators. *New York, Charles Scribner's Sons*, 1892.

SMITH, RALPH CLIFTON, A Biographical Index of American Artists. *Baltimore, The Williams & Wilkins Company*, 1930.

TAFT, LORADO, The History of American Sculpture. *New York, The Macmillan Company*, 1930.

TUCKERMAN, HENRY T., American Artist Life, *New York, G. P. Putnam's Sons*, 1882.

VAN DYKE, JOHN C., American Painting and Its Tradition. *New York, Charles Scribner's Sons,* 1919.

WEITENKAMPF, FRANK. American Graphic Art. *New York,* 1912.

WORKS ON INDIVIDUAL ARTISTS

Bellows—EGGERS, GEORGE W., George Bellows. *New York, Whitney Museum of American Art,* 1931.

——George Bellows, His Lithographs; compiled by Emma S. Bellows. *New York and London, Alfred A. Knopf,* 1928.

Blakelock—DAINGERFIELD, ELLIOTT, Ralph Albert Blakelock. *New York, Privately printed (by F. F. Sherman),* 1914.

Cassatt—WATSON, FORBES, Mary Cassatt. *New York, Whitney Museum of American Art,* 1932.

Chase—ROOF, KATHARINE METCALF, The Life and Art of William Merritt Chase. *New York, Charles Scribner's Sons,* 1917.

Davies—CORTISSOZ, ROYAL, Arthur B. Davies. *New York, Whitney Museum of American Art,* 1931.

Duveneck—HEERMANN, NORBERT, Frank Duveneck. *Boston and New York, Houghton Mifflin Company,* 1918.

Eakins—GOODRICH, LLOYD, Thomas Eakins, His Life and Work. *New York, Whitney Museum of American Art,* 1933.

——The Museum of Modern Art, Winslow Homer, Albert P. Ryder, Thomas Eakins. *New York, The Museum of Modern Art,* 1930.

French—ADAMS, ADELINE, Daniel Chester French. *Boston and New York, Houghton Mifflin Company,* 1932.

Fuller—MILLET, JOSIAH B., editor, George Fuller, His Life and Works. *Boston and New York, Houghton Mifflin Company,* 1886.

Hassam—Childe Hassam; compiled by Nathaniel Pousette-Dart, with an introduction by Ernest Haskell. *New York, Frederick A. Stokes Company,* 1922.

Henri—HENRI, ROBERT, The Art Spirit. *Philadelphia and London, J. B. Lippincott Company,* 1930.

——Robert Henri, His Life and Works; edited by William Yarrow and Louis Bouché. *New York, Privately printed by Boni & Liveright,* 1921.

Homer—DOWNES, WILLIAM HOWE, The Life and Works of Winslow Homer. *Boston and New York, Houghton, Mifflin Company,* 1911.

Inness—INNESS, GEORGE, JR., Life, Art and Letters of George Inness. *New York, The Century Co.,* 1917.

La Farge—CORTISSOZ, ROYAL, John La Farge; a memoir and a study. *Boston and New York, Houghton Mifflin Company,* 1911.

Luks—CARY, ELIZABETH LUTHER, George Luks. *New York, Whitney Museum of American Art,* 1931.

Martin—MATHER, FRANK JEWETT, Homer Martin, Poet in Landscape. *New York, Privately printed (by F. F. Sherman),* 1912.

Prendergast—BREUNING, MARGARET, Maurice Prendergast. *New York, Whitney Museum of American Art,* 1931.

Ryder—PRICE, FREDERIC NEWLIN, Albert Pinkham Ryder. *New York, William Edwin Rudge,* 1932.

Sargent—DOWNES, WILLIAM HOWE, John S. Sargent. *Boston, Little, Brown & Company,* 1925.

Saint-Gaudens—CORTISSOZ, ROYAL, Augustus Saint-Gaudens. *Boston and New York, Houghton Mifflin Company,* 1907.

Thayer—Abbott H. Thayer; compiled by Nathaniel Pousette-Dart, with an introduction by Royal Cortissoz. *New York, Frederick A. Stokes Company,* 1923.

Twachtman—TUCKER, ALLEN, John H. Twachtman. *New York, Whitney Museum of American Art,* 1931.

Ward—ADAMS, ADELINE, John Quincy Adams Ward. *New York, The National Sculpture Society,* 1912.

Weber—CAHILL, HOLGER, Max Weber. *New York, The Downtown Gallery,* 1930.

Weir—Phillips Memorial Gallery, Julian Alden Weir; an appreciation of his life and works. *New York, E. P. Dutton & Company,* 1922.

Whistler—PENNELL, ELIZABETH ROBINS and JOSEPH, The Life of James McNeill Whistler. *Philadelphia, J. B. Lippincott Company,* 1908.

——WHISTLER, JAMES A. McNEILL, Ten O'Clock. *Portland, Me., Thomas Bird Mosher,* 1920.

——WHISTLER, JAMES A. McNEILL, The Gentle Art of Making Enemies. *New York, G. P. Putnam's Sons,* 1923.

Wyant—CLARK, ELIOT, Alexander Wyant. *New York, Privately printed (by F. F. Sherman),* 1916.

Monographs on contemporary American painters and sculptors may be found in the series published by the Whitney Museum of American Art in New York. Good articles on contemporary American painting and sculpture may be found in the files of *The American Magazine of Art, The Arts, Creative Art,* in various exhibition catalogues published by The Metropolitan Museum, The Museum of Modern Art, the Whitney Museum of American Art and other museums.

LIST OF BUILDINGS

The following lists are representative of the more interesting types of building done in this country since the Civil War. The examples selected are fine and characteristic works of their architects and their periods, although many architects have done equally excellent work which is not listed.

Different periods and types of work are naturally better represented in different parts of the country, as Richardson in Boston and the early skyscraper in Chicago. It has not seemed necessary to call particular attention to specific examples of twentieth century revivalism as there are everywhere prominent buildings which conform admirably to the criteria of correctness and taste and yet are otherwise quite devoid of interest.

Inclusion in these lists does not imply that the buildings listed are masterpieces. Omission from them in most cases may mean no more than that many fine buildings are necessarily unknown to the compilers. Study of several of these buildings from each decade since the Civil War should provide any one with an ample picture of the achievement of American architects.

The buildings are grouped in chronological order under cities. Suburbs and small towns are included under the nearest large city.

ALBANY, N. Y.

H. H. RICHARDSON, New York State Capitol, Senate Chamber, 1876-81.

H. H. RICHARDSON, City Hall, 1880.

BALTIMORE, MD.

McKIM, MEADE & WHITE, St. Peter's Church, St. Paul Street and 22nd Street, 1885-87.

C. L. CARSON, Goucher College Main Building, St. Paul Street between 22nd and 23rd Streets, 1886.

J. E. SPERRY, St. Mark's Lutheran Church, 1897.

BOSTON, MASS.

H. H. RICHARDSON, First Baptist Church, Commonwealth Avenue corner Clarendon, 1870-71.

E. T. POTTER, Harvard Street Church, Brookline, 1871-73.

H. H. RICHARDSON, Trinity Church, Copley Square, 1872-77.

H. H. RICHARDSON, Sever Hall, Harvard University, Cambridge, 1878-80.

H. H. RICHARDSON, Trinity Rectory, 1879-81.

H. H. RICHARDSON, Austin Hall, Harvard University, Cambridge, 1881-83.

H. H. RICHARDSON, Railroad Station, Auburndale, 1881.

H. H. RICHARDSON, Crane Library, Quincy, 1881-82.

McKIM, MEAD & WHITE, Miss May's School (C. A. Whittier House), 270 Beacon Street, 1882-83.

H. H. RICHARDSON, Stoughton House, Brattle Street, corner Ash Street, Cambridge, 1882-84.

H. H. RICHARDSON, Converse Public Library, Malden, 1883-85.

H. H. RICHARDSON, Channing House, northeast corner Chestnut Hill Avenue and Channing Road, Brookline, 1883-85.

H. H. RICHARDSON, Ames Building, Harrison Avenue, 1886-87.

McKIM, MEAD & WHITE, Public Library, 1887-95.

BRISTOL, R. I.

McKIM, MEAD & WHITE, William G. Low House, 1886-87.

BUFFALO, N. Y.

H. H. RICHARDSON, New York State Hospital, Forest and Elmwood Avenues, 1870-80.

LOUIS SULLIVAN, Prudential Insurance Company, Church and Pearl Streets, 1894-95.

FRANK LLOYD WRIGHT, Darwin D. Martin House, 1904.

FRANK LLOYD WRIGHT, Administration Building, Larkin Soap Factory, 1904.

CHICAGO, ILL.

WILLIAM LeBARON JENNEY, Leiter Building I, 200 West Monroe Street, 1879.

H. H. RICHARDSON, Glessner House, 1800 South Prairie Avenue, 1885-1887.

ADLER & SULLIVAN, Auditorium Building, Michigan Avenue at Van Buren Street, 1887-89.

ADLER & SULLIVAN, Walker Warehouse, Market Street between Adams and Quincy Streets, 1888-89.

WILLIAM LEBARON JENNEY, Leiter Building II, now Sears Roebuck & Co., southeast corner, State and Van Buren Streets, 1889-90.

BURNHAM & ROOT, Monadnock Block, 53 West Jackson Street, 1891.

CHARLES B. ATWOOD, Museum of Science and Industry, Jackson Park, 1892. Fine Arts Building, World's Fair.

ADLER & SULLIVAN, Charnley House, 1365 Astor Street, 1892.

ADLER & SULLIVAN, Meyer Building, southwest corner Van Buren and Franklin Streets, 1893.

FRANK LLOYD WRIGHT, Winslow House, Lake Street, River Forest, 1892-93.

LOUIS SULLIVAN, Schlesinger-Mayer Building, now Carson, Pirie & Scott, southeast corner, State and Madison Streets, 1889-1903.

LOUIS SULLIVAN, Gage Building, (facade only), 18 South Michigan Avenue, 1899.

FRANK LLOYD WRIGHT, Willits House, Highland Park, 1901.

FRANK LLOYD WRIGHT, River Forest Tennis Club, corner of Lathrop and Quick Streets, River Forest, 1903.

FRANK LLOYD WRIGHT, Unity Church, corner Kenilworth and Lake Streets, Oak Park, 1905-06. On Forest Avenue near by are several early houses by Frank Lloyd Wright.

FRANK LLOYD WRIGHT, F. J. Baker House, 507 Lake Avenue, Wilmette, 1906.

FRANK LLOYD WRIGHT, Steffens House, 7631 Sheridan Road, 1907.

FRANK LLOYD WRIGHT, Coonley House, 300 Scottwood Road, Riverside, 1907-08.

FRANK LLOYD WRIGHT, Isabel Roberts House, 603 Edgewood Place, River Forest, 1908.

FRANK LLOYD WRIGHT, Robie House, 5757 Woodlawn Avenue, corner 58th Street, 1908-09. Now Women's Dormitory of the Congregational Seminary.

JOHN MEAD HOWELLS and RAYMOND HOOD, Tribune Tower, 1922.

HOWARD T. FISHER, Logan House, Willow Road, Northbrook, near Winnetka, 1934.

CLEVELAND, OHIO

C. F. SCHWEINFURTH, University School Building, Hough Avenue, 1890.

CLAUSS & DAUB, Filling Stations for the Standard Oil Company of Ohio, since 1932.

GRAND RAPIDS, MICH.

FRANK LLOYD WRIGHT, Meyer May House, 450 Madison S. E., 1909.

HARTFORD, CONN.

WILLIAM BURGES, Trinity College, 1874- .

H. H. RICHARDSON, Brown-Thompson Company (Cheney) Building, Main Street, 1875-76.

LOS ANGELES, CALIF.

FRANK LLOYD WRIGHT, Barnsdall House, now California Art Club, Olivehill, Hollywood, 1915.

FRANK LLOYD WRIGHT, Millard House, Prospect Crescent Drive, Pasadena, 1921.

FRANK LLOYD WRIGHT, Freeman House, Hollywood, 1922.

R. M. SCHINDLER, Double House, 235 N. Kings Road, Hollywood, 1923.

RICHARD J. NEUTRA, Lovell House, Hollywood, 1929.

RICHARD J. NEUTRA, House of the architect, 2348 Silverlake Boulevard, 1933.

RICHARD J. NEUTRA, Two-story building, corner Vine Street and Hollywood Boulevard, 1933.

RICHARD J. NEUTRA, Anna Sten House, Santa Monica Canyon, Santa Monica, 1934.

RICHARD J. NEUTRA, Scheyer House, Hollywood, 1934.

MILWAUKEE, WIS.

FRANK LLOYD WRIGHT, Apartments, 27th Street Highland Boulevard, 1912.

FRANK LLOYD WRIGHT, Bogk House, 2420 North Terrace Avenue, 1912.

MINNEAPOLIS, MINN.

L. S. BUFFINGTON, Northwestern Storage Warehouse, 1889.

L. S. BUFFINGTON, Security Bank, 1891.

NARRAGANSETT PIER, R. I.

McKIM, MEAD & WHITE, Casino, 1881-84.

NEW HAVEN, CONN.

RUSSELL STURGIS, Farnam Hall, Yale University, 1869-70.

McKIM, MEAD & WHITE, Glee Club (Third Senior Society) Building, 1883-84.

RUSSELL STURGIS, Lawrence Hall, Yale University, 1884-86.

J. C. CADY, CHITTENDEN HALL, Yale University, 1889.

BABB, COOK & WILLARD, Ciampolini (Atwater) House, southeast corner Whitney Avenue and Edwards Street, 1892.

NEW LONDON, CONN.

H. H. RICHARDSON, Railroad Station, 1885-87.

NEWPORT, R. I.

H. H. RICHARDSON, Watts Sherman House, Shephard Ave., 1874-75.

McKIM, MEAD & WHITE, Casino, Bellevue Avenue, 1881.

McKIM, MEAD & WHITE, Isaac Bell House, Bellevue Avenue, corner Perry Avenue, 1882-83.

McKIM, MEAD & WHITE, Robert Goelet House, 1883.

McKIM, MEAD & WHITE, Russell (Leroy King) House, Bellevue Avenue, corner Berkeley Avenue, 1885-86.

R. M. HUNT, The Breakers, 1895.

NEW YORK, N. Y.

J. W. KELLUM, Wanamaker Store, Broadway at 9th Street, 1862-.

LEOPOLD EIDLITZ, Drydock Savings Bank, Bowery at 3rd Street, 1876.

McKIM, MEAD & WHITE, Tiffany House, 72nd Street at Madison Avenue, 1882-84.

McKIM, MEAD & WHITE, Villard Houses, Madison Avenue at 50th Street, 1883-85.

BABB, COOK & WILLARD, DeVinne Press Building, 80 Lafayette Street, 1885.

N. LEBRUN & SONS, Metropolitan Life Insurance Building, Madison Square, 1906.

CASS GILBERT, Woolworth Building, 1911-13.

VOORHEES, GMELIN & WALKER, New York Telephone Building, 140 West Street, 1925.

RAYMOND HOOD, Daily News Building, 1930.

RAYMOND HOOD, McGraw-Hill Building, 330 West 42nd Street, 1931.

SHREVE, LAMB & HARMON, Empire State Building, 1931.

R. G. & W. M. CORY, Starrett Lehigh Building, 601 West 26th Street, 1931.

THOMPSON & CHURCHILL, Office building, Lexington Avenue at 57th Street, 1931.

REINHARD & HOFMEISTER; CORBETT, HARRISON & MACMURRAY; HOOD & FOUILHOUX, Rockefeller Center, 1932-1934.

HENRY C. PELTON, Two story building 59th-60th Streets, Madison Avenue, 1934.

HOWE & LESCAZE, Lescaze House, 211 East 48th Street, 1934.

A. LAWRENCE KOCHER, Week-end House, road opposite entrance to Sunken Meadow Park, near Northport, L. I., 1934.

PHILADELPHIA, PA.

FRANK FURNESS, Provident Trust Company, 409 Chestnut Street, 1879.

HOWE & LESCAZE, Philadelphia Saving Fund Society Building, corner 12th and Market Streets, 1931-32.

KASTNER & STONOROV and W. POPE BARNEY, Carl Mackley Houses near Juniata Park, north Philadelphia, 1934.

PITTSBURGH, PA.

H. H. RICHARDSON, Allegheny County Courthouse and Jail, 1884-88.

PRINCETON, N. J.

J. L. FAXON, Dodd Hall, Princeton University, 1890.

PEABODY & STEARNS, Lawrenceville School, Main Building, Lawrenceville, 1885.

PROVIDENCE, R. I.

McKIM, MEAD & WHITE, W. C. Chapin House, 1251 Westminster Street, 1881-82.

SALT LAKE CITY, UTAH

ADLER & SULLIVAN, Dooly Block, 111 West 2nd South Street, 1890-91.

SAN FRANCISCO, CALIF.

WILLIS POLK & CO., Hallidie Building, 1918.

SPRINGFIELD, MASS.

H. H. RICHARDSON, Unity Church, State Street, 1866.

H. H. RICHARDSON, Hampden County Courthouse, Court Square, 1871-73.

W. A. POTTER, South Congregational Church, Maple Street, 1872-73.

CLARENCE LUCE, W. H. Wesson House, 302 Maple Street, 1882-84.

TULSA, OKLA.

FRANK LLOYD WRIGHT, Richard Lloyd Jones House, 1931.

WASHINGTON, D. C.

A. B. MULLET, State War and Navy Department, 1870-.

M. C. MEIGS, Bureau of Pensions, Judiciary Square, 1887.

WORCESTER, MASS.

E. BOYDEN & SON, Boynton Hall and Washburn Machine Shop, Worcester Institute of Technology, 1866.

WARE & VAN BRUNT, Union Passenger Station, Washington Square, 1872-75.

BIBLIOGRAPHY—ARCHITECTURE

The Story of Architecture in America. THOMAS E. TALLMADGE, New York, W. W. Norton, 1927.

American Architecture. FISKE KIMBALL, New York, Bobbs-Merrill, 1926.

Sticks and Stones. LEWIS MUMFORD, New York, Boni & Liveright, 1924.

The Brown Decades. LEWIS MUMFORD, New York, Harcourt, Brace, 1931.

Modern Architecture. HENRY-RUSSELL HITCHCOCK, JR., New York, Brewer, Warren & Putnam, 1929.

Henry Hobson Richardson: the Catalog of an Exhibition. HENRY-RUSSELL HITCHCOCK, JR., New York, Museum of Modern Art, 1935.

Henry Hobson Richardson and His Works. MARIANA GRISWOLD VAN RENSSELAER, Boston, Houghton Mifflin, 1888.

The Autobiography of an Idea. LOUIS H. SULLIVAN, New York, Press of the American Institute of Architecture, Inc., 1924.

An Autobiography. FRANK LLOYD WRIGHT, London and New York, Longmans, Green, 1932.

The International Style: Architecture Since 1922. HITCHCOCK AND JOHNSON, New York, W. W. Norton, 1932.

Modern Architects: the Catalog of an Exhibition of Modern Architecture. ALFRED H. BARR, JR., ed., New York, Museum of Modern Art, 1932.

Towards a New Architecture. LE CORBUSIER, London and New York, Payson & Clarke, 1928.

BIBLIOGRAPHY—AMERICAN STAGE DESIGN

BROWN, J. M. Upstage. New York, W. W. Norton, 1930.

CHENEY, SHELDON. The Art Theatre. New York, Alfred A. Knopf, 1925.

——— Stage Decoration. New York, John Day Company, 1928.

———Three Thousand Years of Drama, Acting and Stagecraft. New York, Longmans Green & Company, 1929.

The Development of Scenic Art and Stage Machinery. A bibliography compiled by W. B. Gamble. New York Public Library, 1920.

GEDDES, NORMAN-BEL. A Project for a Theatrical Presentation of the Divine Comedy of Dante. New York, Theatre Arts, Inc., 1924.

GREGOR, J. and FÜLÖP-MILLER, R. Das amerikanische Theater und Kino. Vienna, Amalthea, 1931.

HUME, S. J. and FUERST, W. R. Twentieth Century Stage Decoration. New York, Alfred A. Knopf, 1929.

JONES, ROBERT EDMOND. Drawings for the Theatre; with an introduction by Arthur Hopkins. New York, Theatre Arts, Inc., 1925.

MACGOWAN, KENNETH. Footlights across America. New York, Harcourt, Brace and Company, 1929.

———The Theatre of Tomorrow. New York, Boni & Liveright, 1921.

MACKAYE, PERCY. Epoch: The Life of Steele Mackaye; Vol. II. New York, Boni & Liveright, 1927.

MODERWELL, H. K. The Theatre of Today. New York, John Lane Company, 1926.

SELDON, S. and SELLMAN, H. D. Stage Scenery and Lighting. New York, F. S. Crofts & Company, 1930.

SIMONSON, LEE. The Stage Is Set. New York, Harcourt, Brace and Company, 1932

SIMONSON, LEE and others. International Exhibition of Theatre Art. New York, The Museum of Modern Art, 1934.

Stage Scenery; A List of References to Illustrations Since 1900. A bibliography compiled by W. B. Gamble. New York Public Library, 1917.

Theatre Arts Monthly. New York, Theatre Arts, Inc., 1916-date.

BIBLIOGRAPHY—PHOTOGRAPHY IN THE UNITED STATES

AGHA, M. F. Ralph Steiner. Creative Art, Vol. X, No. 1, Jan., 1932.

The American Annual of Photography. New York, 1887-1934.

American Photography. Boston, 1907-date.

American Pictorial Photography; 2 vols. New York, The Camera Club, 1899-1900.

ARMITAGE, M. Art of Edward Weston. Creative Art, Vol. XII, No. 5, May, 1933.

BOUGHTON, ALICE. Photographing the Famous. New York, The Avondale Press, 1928.

BRADY, MATTHEW B. A Photographic History of the Civil War. New York, Review of Reviews Corporation, 1911.

BRUEHL, ANTON. Photographs of Mexico. New York, Delphic Studios, 1933.

CLURMAN, H. Photographs by Paul Strand. Creative Art, Vol. V, No. 4, Oct., 1929.

EASTMAN KODAK COMPANY. Abridged Scientific Publications from the Research Laboratory of the Eastman Kodak Company. Rochester, N. Y., 1913-19.

Edward Weston. New York, E. Weyhe, 1932.

FLATO, CHARLES. Matthew B. Brady, 1823-1896. Hound & Horn, Vol. VII, No. 1, Oct.-Dec., 1933.

GENTHE, ARNOLD. Isadora Duncan; twenty-four studies. New York and London, M. Kennerley, 1929.

The Julien Levy Galleries. Exhibition catalogues: Berenice Abbott, Matthew B. Brady, Walker Evans, Man Ray, etc.

KOOTZ, S. M. Edward J. Steichen. Creative Art, Vol. X, No. 5, May, 1932.

———Ford Plant Photos of Charles Sheeler. Creative Art, Vol. VIII, No. 4, Apr., 1931.

Modern Photography. London, The Studio, Ltd., New York, William Edwin Rudge, 1931-1933.

Murals by American Painters and Photographers. New York, The Museum of Modern Art, 1932.

RIDGE, L. Paul Strand. Creative Art, Vol. IX, No. 4, Oct., 1931.

SANDBURG, CARL. Steichen, the Photographer. New York, Harcourt, Brace and Company, 1929.

SCHWARZ, HEINRICH. David Octavius Hill. New York, The Viking Press, 1931.

SOBY, JAMES. The Photograhs of Man Ray. New York, Random House, Inc., 1934.

STIEGLITZ, ALFRED, editor and publisher. Camera Work; No. 1-50. New York, 1903-1917.

Articles on Charles Sheeler in The Arts; on Alfred Stieglitz and Edward Weston in The Studio; on Photo-Murals in Architectural Record and Architectural Forum. Photographs in current periodicals such as Vanity Fair, Vogue, Fortune, The New York Times rotogravure section, trade and technical journals, etc.

BIBLIOGRAPHY—THE MOTION PICTURE

MUNSTERBERG, HUGO. The Photoplay: a Psychological Study. New York, Appleton, 1916.

LINDSAY, VACHELL. The Art of the Moving Picture. New and rev. ed. New York, Macmillan, 1922.

BARRY, IRIS. Let's Go to the Movies. New York, Payson & Clarke, 1926.

RAMSAYE, TERRY. A Million and One Nights: a History of the Motion Picture. New York, Simon & Schuster, 1926.

ROTHA, PAUL. The Film Till Now: a Survey of the Cinema. New York, Cape & Smith, 1930.

LEJEUNE, C. A. Cinema. London, Maclehose, 1931.

PUDOVKIN, V. I. Film Technique. Enl. ed. London, Newnes, 1933.

Close Up, published quarterly in London and Geneva 1927-1933.

The Film Society, 56 Manchester Street, London. Programs of performances given monthly eight times a year from October 25th, 1925 until the present time.

Color Plates

I. BELLOWS
Club Night

Courtesy Vanity Fair
Collection John Hay Whitney, New York

II. HOPPER
Lighthouse at Two Lights

Courtesy Vanity Fair
Collection Mrs. Samuel A. Tucker, New York

III. KUHN
THE BLUE CLOWN

Courtesy Vanity Fair
Whitney Museum of American Art, New York

IV. SPEICHER
Babette

Courtesy Vanity Fair

V. STERNE
GIRL IN BLUE CHAIR

Collection Mr. and Mrs. Samuel A. Lewisohn, New York

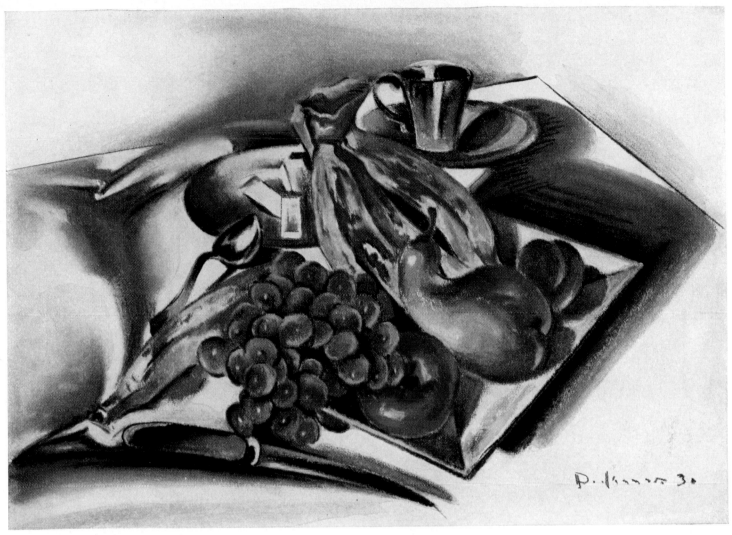

VI. DICKINSON
STILL LIFE

Courtesy Raymond & Raymond, Inc.
Collection Morton R. Goldsmith, New York

VII. MARIN
PERTAINING TO STONINGTON, MAINE

VIII. BURCHFIELD
TILE ROOF

Courtesy Raymond & Raymond, Inc.
Frank K. M. Rehn Gallery, New York

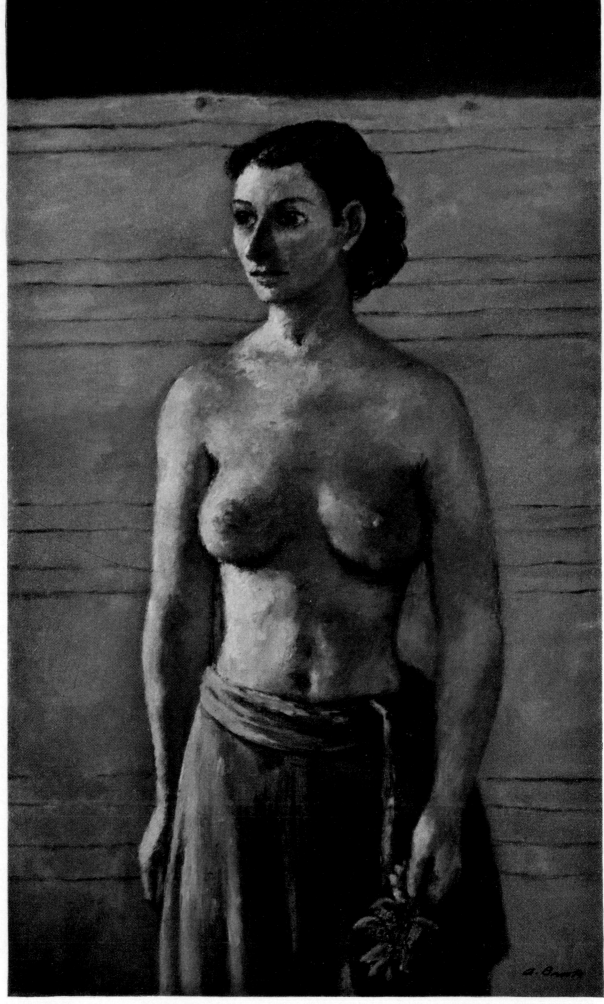

IX. BROOK
Isis

Courtesy Vanity Fair
The Downtown Gallery, New York